Praise for *The 11 Pillars of Self-Realization*

"*The 11 Pillars of Self-Realization* is a beautiful spiritual manual for life! The book does a wonderful job of intertwining 11 life lessons to help all of us live a more understanding and accepting life. I wish everyone was required to read this book because I truly believe we'd have a more peaceful existence. No matter your background one can appreciate the lessons Mitra speaks so effortlessly about. You don't need to be a believer of any kind or have any spiritual constitution to read this book—you just need to be open to having your mind blown."

—Kelli Miller, LCSW—Author of *Love Hacks: Simple Solutions to Your Most Common Relationship Issues*

"Mitra is a light dancer sharing lusciousness wherever she is. This book is an extension of that. Allow this book to be your guide into the pillars that hold you, so you can behold yourself, and know that the Universe has your back, even in the darkest of times. You will have a new tool kit to support you in embracing the true pillars of life. And you will feel wrapped in that light and love we all so deeply desire. Dive in and find the essence of you."

—Gurutej Khalsa—Spiritual Teacher, Author of *Empower Your Essence*. Founder of Empowered Energy Academy

"This lovely book is like embarking on an extended guided meditation with Mitra. It draws the reader into a fully experiential process. She has accomplished the difficult task of making spiritual concepts real and grounded, giving examples from daily life to illustrate her explanations. She also gives the reader simple, practical ways to incorporate meditative practices into a daily rhythm. Neuroscience research is increasingly showing us that meditation can rewire our brains, and can help with recovery from trauma as well as other medical and mental health conditions. I would heartily recommend this book to anyone wanting to begin or expand their contemplative practice."

—Catherine Scott, MD—Trauma Psychiatrist, Assistant Professor of Clinical Psychiatry, USC Keck School of Medicine. Author of *Principles of Trauma Therapy: A Guide to Symptoms, Evaluation, and Treatment*

"Mitra Rahbar is a descendant and student of the great mystical tradition, a healer who uses parables to bypass the conscious mind and help those in her charge navigate the many-layered journey from introspection to transformation. In the great mythological tradition, Mitra connects her own personal narrative to the stories of an adventurous young man, Abu, who is seeking to learn the secrets of life and inner peace, represented by 11 pillars. This is not a book of affirmations or practical steps for personal success. This is rather an opportunity to be led by a magical story that, as it unfolds, takes you exactly where you need to go, without a map, and without a five-year plan. Take the journey. Don't ask for directions. Allow yourself—like Abu—to be tired, hungry, wet, and lost as you tumble down the ravine and then find yourself sitting under the gushing waterfall that cleanses and purifies, giving you strength to complete your soul's mission. Allow yourself as much time and self-care as needed. If you are willing to be led, no questions asked, you will be eternally grateful for this book."

—Ruth Broyde Sharone—Filmmaker/Journalist, Creator of *Meet Me There, The Interfaith Musical*

The 11 Pillars of Self-Realization

The 11 Pillars of Self-Realization

Your Roadmap to Inner Peace

Mitra Rahbar

Copyright ©2024 Mitra Rahbar

No part of this book may be reproduced or transmitted in any form or by any means, electronic or mechanical, including photocopying, recording, or any information storage and retrieval system without written permission from the publisher, except for the inclusion of brief quotations in a review.

All rights reserved.

Zemzemeh Publishing
17216 Saticoy Street #132
Van Nuys, CA 91406

Cover and Interior Design: Morgane Leoni
Author Photo: Rama Morovati
Cover Illustration: Paisorn / Adobe Stock / Generated with AI
Editor: Bobby Rock

Official Site: www.voiceofmitra.com

First Printing 2024
ISBN: 979-8-9909801-0-5

*In honor of my teacher, mentor, and
soul partner in this journey of life,
my beloved mother, Mehrtaj Safai~
for your poetry, teachings, and wisdom,
for your inspiration and everlasting love.*

*Your light shines ever so brightly, forever
guiding my way ...*

"The supreme calling of every human being is to aspire to self-realization. All other obligations are secondary."
Anandamayi Ma

Table of Contents

Introduction	10
Preface	12
Chapter One: Faith	14
Chapter Two: Patience	29
Chapter Three: Vulnerability	45
Chapter Four: Purification	61
Chapter Five: Love	76
Chapter Six: Devotion	92
Chapter Seven: Service	107
Chapter Eight: Wisdom	118
Chapter Nine: Gratitude	131
Chapter Ten: Surrender	145
Chapter Eleven: Unity	159
Epilogue	171
Resources	172
Servants of Love	175
Acknowledgments	176
About the Author	178

Introduction

It was magically revealed ...

The unfolding of *The 11 Pillars of Self-Realization* had been aligned by the stars, with my soul's journey. As I wrote this book, an energy channeled through me ... a whisper through the ancient footages of time: sacred hymns and sweet melodies that awakened my heart to a profound joy on this glorious sail.

And so it is, that the journey I embarked on decades ago was my "resalat": my soul's mission, to be of service. A mystic at heart, I've carried my mission in my everyday life as a guide, healer, and teacher.

Years of prayer, meditation, self-work, and healing brought me further to understand each of our soul's journeys. My mother's knowledge on the Dervish/Sufi philosophy, coupled with my own work and life practice, gave me insight into our inner world. Studying various doctrines, working with thousands of people from all walks of life, and teaching in Iran, the US, and other regions globally, helped me come to an even deeper understanding of our spiritual essence.

Prior to writing *Miraculous Silence*, I had envisioned this book. At that time, it did not have a name or shape. It has only been in the last four years that I have understood exactly what my second book should be—how to build the inner fortress. *Miraculous Silence* was my heart, whereas *The 11 Pillars* is my life's work.

My belief is that all of us will experience these pillars as we seek a life of deeper meaning, peace, and joy. It is then up to us to walk through them, gain that wisdom, and then incorporate them into the grain of our daily lives.

As an immigrant, and a person who was torn from the bosom of her family at barely the age of seventeen, I have learned that there is a glory to each fall, for it is in this that we awaken. And once we do, we have the choice to walk through this beautiful garden and see all that will delight our being and bring us healing, peace, and much joy.

I continue this journey each day as I teach and learn, and as I fall, I lean on the pillars of faith, devotion, vulnerability, and wisdom. As I feel uncertain, I remember patience and surrender. As I get disheartened, I practice gratitude and service, and embrace unity. And when I need to restore, I look to purification and love. The pillars, each one, hold the inner sanctuary intact. In this, there is a liberation like no other, for once the inner fortress is built, it will never crumble. It is there throughout our journey, through the falls, the pauses, and the walk. This is invaluable.

Written in a universal style, my hope is that *The 11 Pillars* will be a valuable guide for all. There are teachings, stories, exercises, practices, and poetic prayers to give you the tools necessary on this most intricate path. This, combined with the parallel fictional story of the young Abu—a seeker of Truth finding his way to each pillar—creates what I hope is a most immersive experience. As Abu arrives and receives the teachings in each pillar, we come to a deeper understanding of ourselves and the Universe. In Abu, we see each part of our being: the seeker, the student, and ultimately, the teacher.

I have chosen animals or elements of nature as the entity of each pillar. This further supports our daily journey to connect with the Earth and one another, and to remember how much we can learn from *all* precious things in our world.

May *The 11 Pillars of Self-Realization* awaken you to you, and to the wisdom teachings of our Universe. May it be your roadmap to inner peace, and may it connect you to the unseen wonders of this magical place we call home. And finally, may it support you to embrace your flight with ease, grace, and joy.

This is my hope and prayer.

With Belief and Heart,
Mitra Rahbar

Preface

Abu sat down. He took a deep breath in. He had journeyed far. The road was rugged and winding. At times, Abu thought he may fall off the rocky cliffside turns. He was starting to get anxious. *When will this end?* It seemed that it had been several weeks since he had begun this journey. His bug-bitten body was tired, thirsty, and hungry. He had brought food and water, but he was being careful with it. He so hoped this would be worth it!

It was now dusk. The breeze was cool. The rough terrain had evened out and the air had started to change. The sky was painted in pink and orange. He saw rabbits jumping and deer prancing. The river was singing melodically, and the birds were harmonizing with it. *What is this enchanted land?* he wondered.

Mesmerized, he walked amongst the ancient trees. Their colossal branches were outstretched through the early night skyline. Soon, he found himself standing in front of an old wooden door. He hoped this was the entrance to the pillars: the site of his coveted destination.

With excitement, Abu took in a deep breath. As he tried to open the door, he noticed a large iron key in the lock. He instinctively turned it. The heavy door slowly swung open with a creaky sound. He stepped in. A foggy haze hung in the air. He could sense an endless vastness, although he could not see too far in front of him. He felt an energy he could not describe, but one that felt so good to him. He took a few steps forward. An old man was sitting on a large rock, holding a walking stick. Abu went to him.

"Salam," he said.

"As-salam, my son," the man replied, looking up at him with small, beady eyes.

"Baba ... is this the way to the pillars?"

"Yes, my son, it is."

"But where are they? I mean ... how do I find them?" Abu asked.

The man chuckled.

"Do you want to find them?" he asked.

What an odd question, thought Abu.

"Yes, I do, I have traveled far to do so," he replied.

"And who told you of these pillars?" the old man asked.

Abu was silent for a few seconds. He knew he had to tell the truth, but the old man would think he was crazy!

"To be honest, Baba," said Abu, "I dreamt of them."

The old man smiled, as his eyebrows slightly lifted in amusement. He looked up at Abu, observing him for a second. "How did you know where to come to find them?" he asked.

"I just followed the signs," said Abu.

The old man's eyes twinkled.

"You will be fine. Just follow the signs," said the old man. He then got up and disappeared into the vastness.

Abu wanted to go after him, as the old man had forgotten to take his walking stick. But the haze had thickened.

Abu looked around. He couldn't see very well. He had been called to this since he had dreamt it almost a year ago. He took the walking stick and slowly proceeded. He had to have faith that he would find what he had been searching for.

Chapter One

Faith

Abu walked through the misty fog. He hoped he was walking in the right direction. His narrow path through the woods was illuminated by the soft glow of the moon. He suddenly stopped. There it was, several meters away, so majestic. A cylinder-shaped cluster of stars. Brilliant, full of light. It was a stunning sight! It took his breath away.

He slowly approached it. It lit up the night air with a magical radiance. A deep sense of joy and wonderment filled his heart.

"I wonder what this is?" he thought out loud.

Just then, a single star twirled forth and danced around his head.

"You are at the Pillar of Faith," it whispered.

"Faith?" asked Abu. "Is that the first pillar?"

The star swirled around him again and said, "Yes, it is ... before all else."

"What do you mean 'before all else'?" Abu asked.

"I mean it's been here within you, before you were even born," the star explained.

A feeling awakened in Abu.

"Can you tell me more about this Pillar of Faith?" he asked.

"Yes," said the star. As it began to read from the book, *The 11 Pillars of Self-Realization*, the other stars gathered around.

And thus ... the teachings began.

THE TEACHINGS

"Faith is an oasis in the heart which will never
be reached by the caravan of thinking."
Kahlil Gibran

It feels like the doors are shut with no way out.

My thoughts spin. I am penniless. I have no visa, no housing, no place to stay, and a kidney infection with a high fever. My boyfriend, who is also my best friend, is stuck across the ocean as his visa to enter the United States has been denied.

Panic starts setting in. It takes over my reasoning, my emotions. I am breathing fast. I feel like I'm trying not to drown as the waves are crashing against me.

And yet, I fight for something ... something to hold on to ... an anchor. I have no clue what will happen, but somewhere deep inside of me, at the young age of only twenty-six, I know it comes down to one thing—I have to believe in the wisdom of the Universe, trust that I am being watched over, and have faith that, although the doors appear to be closed, a window will open. Somewhere deep inside of me, my soul believes this. I know it does. Now I have to. And I will. I have to walk into this belief. This is the only choice my soul can accept.

What Is the Inner Fortress without Faith?

When we build the foundation of a house, we cement the first pillar: this is the king pillar, or the central pillar, integral to holding up the entire house. This pillar is faith, and it is intertwined with the attributes of belief and trust. In building the inner fortress—a sanctuary for the soul—we cannot construct the foundation if this pillar does not exist. For in the absence of faith, all the other pillars will bend and sway.

Faith has many layers and encompasses much more than its five letters. It is one of the essential ingredients to anything of substance in life. It is key in our relationships, in our confidence and convictions, and in our challenges and resolutions. Faith is what the wind is to a bird; it trusts that the winds will lift its wings to take off and fly as it soars into the endless skies.

Whether we believe in an entity called God, Nature, or the Cosmos, faith connects us from the seed of our soul to the seed of the Universe. Without faith, there is a tremendous void in our journey to self-realization. Imagine a tree. How can it stand strong if it is not connected to its roots?

In my practice of close to four decades, I have encountered many people who, from a very young age, said they had always felt a deep faith, presence, and connection to the Universe—something beyond their physical existence. This was defined to them in various ways, such as God, Nature, or even as the "Great Unseen." They said they never doubted It and had complete trust in It.

I have also heard the exact opposite: those who said they never felt such a connection or, if they did, they questioned Its validity. This is where the subject of faith as a belief in an entity outside of ourselves gets muddled.

I cannot tell you how many times I have been asked to show a person what faith is. Whether it was about a Creator or a belief in the Great Unseen, my answer through the decades has been the same: Faith is what you do not always see, but which is fully present in each moment. If in this reference we are talking about a spiritual entity, I say It exists in all spaces, up or down, east or west. But it must be believed, since it cannot be proven as a tangible entity any more than love or kindness can. It is a feeling, a belief, a knowing. Faith just is.

As people question faith, they are often looking for a logical, scientific explanation. In truth, however, all spiritual principles are experienced by the soul's inner knowing. It is not through the eyes of the mind that we can see this, but through the "eyes of the heart." This is faith, and it can be fully obtained once we relinquish the need to prove it. Perhaps Einstein said it best: "The more I study science, the more I believe in God."

Starting with Trust

Faith is to spiritual realization as breath is to the body. And trust, as an indispensable sub-pillar to faith, is often a good place to begin this building process.

Is trust innate? How do we develop it? Why do we lose trust at times? Why are some people more trustful than others? Is trusting the Universe more important than trusting ourselves?

These are all valid questions that we have likely asked ourselves at numerous times along our life's journey. Let's explore all of these questions and more as we begin to unwrap the deep and layered subject of trust.

In the Beginning

When we were infants held in our parents' arms, we learned to trust that a warm embrace, a feeding schedule, and our favorite blanket were reliable aspects of our daily reality. We would simply cry when we needed something, and the food, the hug, or the warmth would soon appear. At this stage of our earthly existence, it was in our nature to trust. And fortunately, for most of us, there was usually someone around to answer our pleadings, which only served to reinforce this innate trust.

This is similar to the trust relationship we have with the Universe. From a very young age, many of us have known or felt a presence of something much greater than ourselves that we may call God or the Universe. In this Great Unseen, we have put our trust. After all, this omnipotent Source has created the entire Earth and all known galaxies, and has governed them for billions of years. It has fine-tuned everything to the height of brilliance and beauty, through science and design, from the colors of flowers and the shapes and sizes of all living beings, to the varied landscapes, oceans, and shifting seasons. And It has never failed to gift the skies, moon, sun, or stars with perfect synchrony. So, this Source, which is also *our* Creator, is obviously looking over and protecting us. Our trust in this Great Unseen is absolute … or so we hope.

A Common Fall from Grace

But then something happens along the way, usually in our teen or young adult years. We face the challenges in this school of life, and we fall, we make mistakes, we get disappointed, and our dreams, at times, shatter. It seems things are turning out differently than we had hoped. At this juncture—unlike in our infancy—we are not getting our way and we feel someone or something did not show up for us, so we pull back. We start questioning the wisdom of the Universe. We start doubting that the Universe is protecting or looking after us, and that is where our trust gets tarnished. But it is also exactly at this point when we need to examine more closely, and understand with deeper insight, the relationship between ourselves and the Universe.

One of our main issues here is we are approaching our trusting of the Universe somewhat similarly to trusting a person. We are testing It, in a way. We are saying, *Show up for me and do what I want or else!* But here are a few key points that are critical to understand:

- A person can come and go in our life. The Universe is constant from before this incarnation to after. It is there every second of each day. It never leaves.

- Contrary to a person, who can hurt us, the Universe does not punish or betray us. It has no ego and no agenda. The nature of the Universe is all loving because, when it comes to the Universe, the very nature of creating is birthed out of pure love.

- Many of our human relationships are based to some degree on mutual understandings. By contrast, we don't share this same kind of arrangement with the Universe. It is not here to do things we want It to do.

Getting Back on Track with Trusting

We are in this school of life to grow, serve, elevate and, hopefully, find joy throughout the journey. We are here, in this world, after all, to create a life of meaning. We are not here to test the Gods, the seasons, or the stars. We are here, instead, to use each of those components as a guide and to learn from the wisdom of Existence (or *Hasti*, a Persian word that means "all that is").

For us to not trust the Universe is like saying we do not trust that the day will birth the sun, or the night will birth the moon. We cannot deny the presence of the moon, stars, and sun. They exist and come out in a timely manner, no matter what. Everything in Existence is governed by a uniquely perfect sort of calibration, and nothing can affect its plan. So, when we say we do not trust the Universe, we are, in essence, saying we do not honor the Governor of this huge mansion of life.

Still, though, we doubt the Divine Order. In fact, we sometimes even go as far as to assign blame to the Universe. As humans we make mistakes and poor judgment calls, and then when things don't go the way we prefer, we don't want to take responsibility because that will mean we need to look inside and say, *This one is on me*. Instead, we try to blame someone else, and when there is no one else to blame, we blame "the Universe"!

Of course, in many instances, there is no one and nothing to blame. Life is full of trials and challenges, and sometimes things don't happen the way we want for reasons we may never fully understand. And yet, many of us find a false sense of comfort in blaming the Universe, since it takes focus off something else at play: the idea that we don't trust ourselves.

Trust Is a Choice

In stumbling and falling we have two choices: one is to not trust what has happened and constantly question the flow and wisdom before us. The other is to trust it and believe the experience is for our growth and evolution, and ultimately, for our wholeness in this physical world.

At seventeen, I was waiting at the embassy with hundreds of others for a visa to the US. I did not want to leave my country and family, but my mother thought it would be best for my education to leave, as there was much political turmoil, and my school would soon close. I prayed hard and asked God to please *not* grant me a visa. But out of the hundreds who were denied, my application was accepted, and there it was: a stamp on my passport! I was stunned. It was clear that the Universe had a different plan for me. Of course, at seventeen, I did not understand it and it very much frustrated me. But, years later, as my country was rattled with war and so much unrest, I understood that the Universe had my back and had guided me.

So, you see, trust is a choice. To not trust makes us feel as if we have control, which gives us a false sense of security. But, in truth, we hardly have any control in life, since control is in itself an illusion. We cannot control the winds or rain, we cannot foresee accidents, and we cannot control the reaction of others. And as we "hold our fist tightly" around things in an effort to wield control, we create barriers to trusting the Universe's wisdom, as well as trusting that we have that wisdom within us.

Therefore, it is up to us to relinquish this tendency to grip tightly to things beyond our control. And as our fists open, we can feel the tingling sensation in each finger, feel the breeze awaken our senses, and open ourselves up to more wholly embrace the righteous flow of the Universe.

Inward and Onward

Many people trust the wisdom of the Universe, but when it's time for them to take action on something in their own life, they cannot trust their own mind and heart to make a decision. This can stem from many things, such as past experiences, fear of making wrong choices, or lack of confidence or self-love. But if we trust the Universe, we need to find that trust within ourselves, for we have that same goodness, wisdom, and light within us.

A man I know in his early forties kept questioning each decision he made. He was often paralyzed to take action in his life. I later found out when he was a child, he was constantly admonished by his parents. This resulted in him not believing in himself as a young boy, which led to him having major trust issues as an adult.

Another woman I know dealt with similar issues, but arrived at them very differently. She had been given everything on a "silver spoon" through most of her life, not unlike an infant whose desires are immediately attended to. When her financial situation changed, her privileges eventually dried up. After a few years, her energies were so depleted that she no longer trusted that the Universe would ever bring her anything. And since she never thought she was capable of creating her own abundance, she had never developed the trust in herself to see her own light to move forward.

Trusting ourselves, trusting the Universe, and trusting the relationship we have with the Great Unseen is a huge pillar of the inner fortress. Most of us trust ourselves in shallow waters, but not always in the deeper ones. Can this level of self-trust really be achieved? One hundred percent! Does it take long? Not necessarily. But you have to "trust" that you can achieve it.

If Trust Is a Choice, Then Faith Is a Must

Each person has a different experience of how they feel or sense the enormity of the Universe and its Unseen Forces. To some, It resides in nature—the mother of all. To others, It is simply an energy they cannot define. No matter what name we give It, we cannot deny that, in our depth, we feel something much bigger than us is present. Once we find this belief, it strengthens as we embrace it more and more in our daily life. Faith is not only a belief, or a decision to trust, but it is a way of being, for it is carried out in our daily life—the faith of knowing, the faith of believing, the faith of loving, of doing. Faith is a conduit of sorts; it is the connector of us to the Beyond.

When I was seven years of age, my younger sister, who was just a few months old, got a cold with a high temperature. My mother looked concerned, so I decided to camp out on the floor in her bedroom as my baby sister was sleeping in my mother's bed. In the middle of the night, I woke up crying, thinking I was going to lose my baby sister. I vividly remember feeling such a sense of desperation, and needing so deeply to connect to something. I closed my eyes and felt a big energy within and around me, and I started praying and praying until I fell asleep.

In the morning, my sister was better, but what had happened changed my life from that point forward. In that moment of raw vulnerability and desperation, I had turned inward and felt a presence, a light, an anchor. And I understood deep in my soul, that that which I called God, or Light, did exist, for I could feel It, and even see It with my inner eye. That experience was the birth of a deep knowing and belief in my life. From that moment forward, the Light literally held me, and I went to Its altar many more days and nights.

Believe!

When a deeper level of knowledge and truth is present on a soul level, we believe, and the vibrational frequency of our faith is stronger and more palpable. In this way, belief has a magical resonance to it, for it is truly about that emotional and spiritual connection to faith and trust. After all, what is our world without the magical resonance of belief? It is the brilliance that propels us forward, inspires us, motivates us, and at times has us dance through the horizons of our journey.

Belief also stems from the possibilities the soul has awakened to when the mind is receptive. When we believe in something or someone, we feel no pause, and that is why it is magical, for it is about the leap of faith that the soul just willingly takes; it is about surrendering to this understanding that we are flying on the wings of our belief. Without this belief, our faith and trust in something will waver. This is why a pessimist has a hard time believing that things can work out: they have never been awakened to belief.

Can our beliefs be strengthened? Yes, for as our trust and faith find deeper anchors within us, we will start feeling the rise of our belief in ourselves and in the Divine Order. This belief will support us in residing more in the light of our being, our joy, and our confidence. And ultimately, we will come to know our spiritual soul and connect with the Unseen Forces.

As a practice, faith opens the pathway of realization, of living a life of truth, purity, intention, patience, belief, trust, kindness, self-love, and awareness. This, in time, becomes the walk … the way. As a "peaceful warrior," we learn this walk, and live in accordance with each "faith step" we take. No longer will the steps mislead us, or the setbacks keep us down, for we have understood through the wisdom of these great pillars that our inner sanctuary is built on faith, and from thereon we stand strong with these pillars. And with this belief and trust, we will always find our way.

Developing Faith in Yourself

Here are a few exercises and practices you can try weekly to develop more trust in your relationship with yourself:

- Close your eyes and take a few steps around a room in your home. You may get anxious or bump into a table or chair, but in time you will learn to trust your senses and find your way.

- On a piece of paper, write, *I am not the harsh critic, I am the loving parent.* Any time you are hard on yourself, remember these words. This will strengthen your inner trust and self-love.

- Practice trusting your higher wisdom by making smaller decisions more often. Whether they work out or not, learn from the experience. The real value with this practice is that you are taking baby steps to build inner trust.

- Do a simple mantra daily: *I trust the Universe—I trust myself—we are intertwined.*

- When you want to make a bigger decision about something, sit with it for a while. Then close your eyes, and see which option resonates better with your soul.

Developing Faith in the Universe

Here are a few exercises and practices you can try weekly to develop more trust in your relationship with the Universe:

- Repeat daily: *I trust Your wisdom.*

- Pay attention to nature. See all of her intricacies and miracles daily.

- Connect to the sound of your breath with the mantra, *Ham Sa*, which means, "I am that." This will allow you to feel part of all there is.

- Meditate or pray without asking for anything. Just be present.

Note: For more information on mantra or meditation practice, go to the Resources section at the end of the book.

In Faith, we find godliness and goodness, we find belief and trust. And once this is cemented, it will only anchor and support us. Faith is all-encompassing ... the forever light that shines on.

〜

O Great Unseen ...
As I stand before You,
I feel Your light within me ...
Your love fills each corner of my being,
and in this,
I trust.
I trust in that which is before me,
and in all that will unfold ...
Anchored in this belief,
I shall always reside.
With this faith,
I shall walk each day.
Knowing the home for which I have searched
lies within me.
In each breath and in each step,
it shall forever remain.

〜

Abu sat quietly, absorbing all he had just heard. He had a question. As soon as he came to voice it, he was stopped.

"Believe," said the star.

Abu closed his eyes. He lay down at the foot of the Pillar of Faith. A warmth entered his being. He cuddled into it. "Believe," he repeated to himself, as he fell into the most magical of sleeps.

Chapter Two

Patience

Abu woke up at dawn. The sky was magical and full of promise. He sprung to his feet and washed his face in a small pond. He ate a bit of food from his backpack. Excited, he looked down the long road ahead. He could not see where the turns might take him. Undaunted, he grabbed the old man's stick and continued his journey on the narrow dirt trail.

The morning sun was warm. Each passing hour it was getting hotter. At one point, the path steepened sharply. Each time he climbed up, he would slide down. There was no other way through. After several more tries, he finally made it all the way.

An endless desert vastness was upon him. He was getting tired and felt ready to be at the next pillar. The day gave into night, and still there was no sight of any pillar. This continued for days. He felt his patience was getting tested. Frustrated, he gave a big scream out into the barren desert heat, and then continued.

Suddenly, his eyes caught a sight from afar. He saw a large, clay-like dome temple. Was this a pillar? It was inscribed in symbols and images with great precision and intricacy. He sat on a big rock. He could not take his eyes off this magnificent creation. But he was soon distracted.

To his great surprise, he saw an enormous caravan of ants. They were feverishly carrying small pieces of clay to the top of the dome. He slowly got up and walked carefully to the front of the structure. A huge ant was making his way down a wall of the temple.

"Salam," Abu said.

"As-salam," replied the King Ant, hastily.

"Excuse me. Is this a pillar?"

"Yes. This is the Pillar of Patience," said the King Ant, busy focusing on the task of getting clay up the pillar.

"Yes, of course!" said Abu enthusiastically, chuckling. "Can you please tell me about this pillar?" he continued.

"Not now," said the King Ant. "I have work to do. You will have to be patient and wait."

"Ok," said Abu, smiling at the irony of the ant's response.

He waited for hours, but the King Ant remained busy with his task. Abu eventually fell asleep in the heat of the sun.

"Wake up!" he heard the King Ant call to him sometime later. It was almost sundown. "Let us begin."

Abu quickly sat upright. He knew he would need to pay close attention. The King Ant was likely short on time.

Abu listened intently, as the King Ant started reading from *The 11 Pillars*.

THE TEACHINGS

"Knowing trees, I understand the meaning of patience.
Knowing grass, I can appreciate persistence."
Hal Borland

The young woman feels like she is running out of time, even though she is barely thirty.

"I am so behind," she tells me, "nothing is moving. I feel I should be in a much higher position than where I am with my work. Ugh!" she says in frustration. "Why is time going by so fast and I am not accomplishing much? I don't want to be one of those people who finally 'gets it' at forty!"

Smiling, I quietly say to myself, *I have been there. You will learn that the Universe requires patience, for we are here to learn, grow, and walk into true awakenings. And that, my dear, always requires time; it cannot be rushed. The Universe works on its time, not our time.*

I do not voice this out loud, for I know she will not be able to hear me … not now. She will get to this, like all of us, in due time.

It may be surprising for some of you to think of patience as a key pillar, but without it, the soul cannot come into true growth, awareness, or enlightenment. Patience is the fertile ground that allows us to see grace, to become whole, to heal, and to gain wisdom. Patience not only helps us find a more powerful passage to understanding life, but also to our spiritual evolution. As we develop these muscles, we grow by leaps and bounds.

Just as life itself cannot be rushed, neither can our lives. When things seem as if they are stagnant, we grit our teeth and feel we should already be at a different place in our lives. But the truth is—to *become* ready, we need to *get* ready, and this requires patience, allowance of time, healing, and acquiring some insight and wisdom. We think we cannot muster the patience for this, but we can and we will, each one of us. Also, challenges and circumstances that each one of us will experience in our lifetime will require us to be patient. And the Universe helps grant us this patience through living and aging.

Patience is our ally, our friend, a beautiful gift that assists us in awakening into a new light. It helps us transform our pain, deepen our knowledge, and gain wisdom until we can see and appreciate the flow of life and all of its varied rhythms. And with this appreciation, we will actually enjoy being patient and not rushing, for it allows us to see the garden grow, the rains to fall, and the sun to rise.

So, why is patience such a challenge for us in modern-day society? Have we truly become like the child who seeks instant gratification in every moment? Have we lost patience with the process of life itself? What has become of the idea of diligently preparing for the next stage, doing the work, and putting in the hours? Is rushing through life one of the reasons we are more anxious and depressed as a nation, and as a global society?

To answer these questions, we need only to observe the technological and cultural shifts of the past few decades. Let's start at the beginning.

The Culture of Quick

"Patience is a virtue."

How many times have we each heard this and resented it? A friend of mine would always reply to this statement, "Patience is a virtue *that I have none of!*"

When we were teenagers, we hated to wait around for anything. Quotes like the above—or "All good things are worth waiting for"—really got on our nerves, and patience became this ugly bully. We didn't understand why we had to be patient for anything in life.

But then, when we would observe an older person doing a task, we noticed they really took their time, for they had learned one thing that truly can only come with experience; life takes time. This is why we always heard our elders talk of the good old days: "We used to be patient as youngsters, and not like kids today who want everything now." Their point is well taken.

These days, however, it isn't just the youngsters who want everything now. Our insatiable "need for speed" has seeped into every facet of our culture and affected virtually every age group. Our "quicky" society has become so much more time-conscious, and we constantly feel rushed. Half the time (or more) we sit in front of our computers or smartphones and multitask our way through the ever-crowded terrain of the digital world. Our attention spans have shrunk. Reading books has taken a back seat to our daily consumption of bite-sized social media posts. And we are always on the lookout for the next quick fix … a faster way of doing things.

This "everything now" approach has made its way into our daily world of in-person interaction, as well. We feel angst as we stand in line at the post office or bank, or grow impatient if there is a slight delay with an appointment time. We opt for the speed and ease of the fast-food meal versus the home-cooked meal. And even our basic forty-five minutes of exercise at the gym is being threatened by the lure of the latest ten-minutes-at-home "miracle workout" ad—which promises the same results in a fraction of the time.

And yet, can you bake a potato in one minute? No. Can you have a baby after being pregnant three months? No. There are time energies for everything. No matter how much you want to rush through time, the truth is, you cannot. There is a universal order to this madness of life. There is a time for sunrise, a time for sunset, and a time for the stars to fill the night sky. Likewise, we start from point A, then go to B, before we can progress to C. This is the process of our evolution. There cannot be any quick fixes to give us better results.

The fact that there are time energies for everything applies to every facet of our lives. We feel we are ready for love, for example, but most of the time we want it the way we want it, and we are not really open to other visions. I can recall a client who kept calling, emailing, and visiting me with questions about her love life. She always wanted me to say something fantastic was going to happen tomorrow. (Isn't that what we all secretly wish for?) She felt after two years she had been patient long enough and was ready to meet her life partner ... right now. She was giving the Universe an ultimatum—bring me my life partner or else! *Or else nothing*, I thought to myself. *She will have to wait.*

To live a fulfilling life, there are no shortcuts. The route to get there can change, but it cannot be shortened. Going from Los Angeles to New York is a five-plus-hour flight. You can take alternate routes that fly over different cities, but in the end, it still takes over five hours! There are no quick fixes, and no special schemes that will truly deliver a better result, for time has an order, life has an order, and especially, our personal growth has an order.

A Faster Path to Enlightenment?

All of these shifts to a "quicky culture" mentality have not been limited only to our day-to-day routines and activities. We are also looking for quick fixes in the realms of our spiritual, mental, and emotional health.

Should I go to the hypnotherapist, or should I just ask my psychic or astrologer?

One session with my energy worker to have my chakras balanced should do the trick!

Not to dismiss supportive tools for our growth, but in all of my years as a social worker, then intuitive and teacher, I have never known a quick fix for the healing process. Instead, I believe that long-term dedication and commitment to the spiritual self is integral for us to truly embrace the practice of patience. It is only then that we can begin to understand that life works in ways that are essential to help us grow and evolve. And we recognize that certain life events may not be part of *our* plan, but they are part of the plan of the Universe. In this way, patience is a gift we can give ourselves, because it helps the soul find spaces to breathe through and break through. And it is in these spaces that we find new perspectives, clarity, and thus liberation. This helps us go through the challenges of life with more ease and wisdom.

Still, we cannot rush the process for this kind of growth. We can't magically jump ahead a few levels in our evolution as a means of arriving to a more evolved place sooner. This is because the patient, steadfast navigation of the journey itself is a critical factor in the process. Imagine taking a first-grader and suddenly throwing them into a fifth-grade class. Beyond the knowledge gap, we couldn't expect the first-grader to have the mental or emotional maturity to thrive in this more advanced environment. They would really need to progress through the full grade-by-grade process, not just in terms of classroom knowledge, but in all aspects of the experience. This takes time.

The great news is, spiritual practice rooted in patience is always rewarded. This makes it different from other pursuits. You can aspire to achieve certain heights in a career path, or obtain a large amount of wealth. But even with all the patience in the world, there are no assurances you will be rewarded with the outcome you are looking for. With the work you do in the realm of inner growth, however, your efforts are returned to you tenfold.

My Pilgrimage of Patience

Needless to say, I, too, have gotten caught up in this "quicky culture" of wanting things to evolve as fast as possible. At the age of thirty-one, a powerful relationship in my life ended. It felt like the castle of my dreams had collapsed, and that all the pain from my past suddenly came up and took my heart hostage. I felt the pain of being away from family, broken relationships, and loneliness. I knew I had to heal.

I went to a therapist and vividly remember telling him I was a quick learner and only needed a few sessions to heal. He chuckled. As I look back, I'm sure he thought to himself, *A few sessions, huh? Ok, fine ... we will discuss this in six months!* Well, honestly, it took me a long time to heal. The more I delved into my heart and soul, the more I realized how I had survived so much, but had not taken time to process all that had happened. I did not know how; I was busy surviving.

But now, my soul was calling me into this pilgrimage of the self, and it required many things, but mainly, lots of patience: with the mending of my heart, forgiveness of myself and others, acceptance of the hand of fate and my choices. There were no shortcuts, even though I was a student of psychology, a believer, and a quick learner in my own eyes. You see, I had to want to heal and be willing to allow the process to unfold, for this was a big load that I had been carrying. How could it be dumped and forgotten in a minute? It was not possible. And if you do the math, you will find that it takes lots of time to heal from years of pain and disappointment.

And so, as my soul kept nudging me for attention, I decided to dedicate myself to my inner work, and I became a diligent student of my growth and healing. When I would go to a party, I would leave before 11:00 p.m. to do my nightly ritual of meditation and prayer. My friends were in disbelief over this.

"Mitra," they would say, "we're having fun! If you just did your routine last night, why not skip it tonight?"

And I would reply, "You don't skip eating today just because you ate yesterday."

The implication was, of course, that meditation and prayer had become a non-negotiable "food" for my soul, and I required a daily feeding. I'm not sure they quite got the point, but I did. In fact, this process extended over the next few years and became part of my daily life. Eventually, my patience was rewarded; the fears and disappointments subsided and even became invaluable teaching points, and I was able to shed the burden of those deepest wounds as they began to lighten, and then heal.

It did not happen overnight, but clearly, my soul was rewarding me for my patience as I discovered a new way of being, of walking through the world. In those sacred hours of prayer and meditation, I created a deeper bond with myself and the Universe, and walked into a higher spiritual understanding. I felt like I had learned a new language and, while not yet fluent in it, I could see that this new language would help me for the rest of my life ... if I just persisted with it.

Patience and Perseverance: The Hand and Glove

Being patient and persevering with the emotional, physical, mental, and spiritual learning of life helps us to see and understand the realm of the Unseen. It also helps us connect to the light within us, and find not only our own godliness, but the Universal Light: the God we believe in.

This requires constant homework, and to consistently exercise our soul muscles, we have to persist. Perseverance is to patience as the hand is to the glove. One supports the other. Perseverance to the spiritual self helps us endure and transcend the agony, the pain, the trials, and the setbacks of the journey. It coaxes the soul to get up, to believe, to persist, and ultimately, to be patient. Sometimes, we may get impulsive and frustrated. However, if we tune in to that inner realm of wisdom—that we each have—we can understand that our perseverance and patience will result in a more awakened self with a new perception and, therefore, guide us to a more favorable outcome.

In my *Servants of Love* training, I had a student with much on her plate. She had endured a history of psychological challenges, as well as an extended bout with addiction, and now her daughter was struggling with some of these same issues. Additionally, she had become disillusioned with the industry of her lifelong passion and was having to reevaluate what her next career adventure might look like.

Yet, she remained patient, knowing that the spiritual pilgrimage to reclaim her voice and power would take time. She persisted through the pain of discovery, the process of healing, and the dedication to the journey of self-realization. And soon, with admirable perseverance, she came into a beautiful plateau of awakening and healing. Gone was the fearful young woman I had just recently known. She had reclaimed her voice.

This doesn't mean she will not have big challenges and hurdles ahead, but now she has toned those soul muscles. She has learned that to untie knots, heal scars, and overcome challenges requires breathing space and persistence. So, with each lesson, setback, or relapse, she immediately draws on her inner learning of patience and perseverance: treasures she will always be able to access within herself. She will forever have her "toolbox," or "treasure chest," of all the modalities she has learned and awakened to.

Patience vs. Impatience

When we do not exercise patience, we can create many mistakes, setbacks, and even consequences that can reach far into the future. Imagine driving impatiently and rushing through each light or stop sign. We can not only get a ticket, but also risk getting into an accident. And if we become impatient in an argument, we can create hurt feelings and even damage the relationship by saying regrettable things that we really don't mean. Had we simply waited a few seconds, taken a deep breath, and exercised a little patience, we could have possibly resolved the matter. So, remember to take a deep breath and choose patience over impatience!

Also, as we are impatient and feel a need to rush from here to there and do a million things, we cramp our soul, and find it difficult to breathe in the moments. If we rush constantly, in time, we will feel an anxiety, not only with rushing, but also with stillness. For you see, our soul is our sanctuary, and to feed it with a constant barrage of things to rush through, we are sending a message to our mind that stillness is not good for us, as it implies laziness or lack of activity. The opposite is true. As we rush, we neglect to smell the flowers, see the signs, and understand our own inner mechanisms. Patience is the gift our soul needs and craves ... always.

Cultivating Patience

So, how can we become more patient?

I believe with consistent discipline and dedication, our capacity for patience is strengthened. Daily meditation, prayer, yoga, tai chi, walking, cooking, gardening, playing a musical instrument, knitting, sowing, or other concentrated practices help us breathe through the challenging moments, as we understand and embrace the journey and don't become impatient with ourselves. These disciplines help us to understand the beautiful timing of the Universe in our lives. And when we allow for those spaces to just breathe, we actually enjoy being patient and not rushing. Imagine your life as a flower: you want to enjoy every magical phase of the blooming process.

To become more patient and enjoy the allowance of time and space, these exercises will support your journey:

- Each day as you wake up, be aware of your breathing. Sit in stillness for a few seconds and breathe in and out.

- Start your morning with becoming aware of all that is around you: the beauty of the sky, the magnificence of the trees, or the warmth of the sun. Connect to them. Do not rush and check your cell phone or go on the computer. Ease into your day gracefully.

- When you feel rushed, take a step back. Pause. Count to ten, then reframe your steps and actions, mastering your body to not rush.

- At bedtime, close your eyes, and breathe in and out a few times. Feel your heartbeat and tune into the pulse of your body.

- Practice putting all technological devices away each day for thirty minutes to an hour. Read a book, go for a walk, pray, meditate, or just be.

- Every week, spend time preparing at least half of your meals. This will help you cultivate patience.

Look within your heart: there, you will be granted infinite patience if you allow it, and the rewards are more brilliant than diamonds on mountain sands. Through your efforts you will discover a new you, a loving God, and a oneness with the Universe. You will become whole.

〜

O my soul ...
Find your steps
and build your pillar,
brick by brick.
Build with patience.
Build with love.
Build with this belief,
that in time,
when you are truly ready,
you shall arrive.

"What does it mean to become whole?" Abu asked the King Ant. But the ant was already busy again, directing the assembly line. Abu watched them for hours. Their focus and persistence were amazing. He was learning more about patience just from observing them.

It was getting dark. Abu looked up at the blue-black sky, speckled with stars. He could feel a peace within him. He felt no rush, or anxiety. The desert was calm and peaceful. He felt connected to his surroundings. *Is this the feeling of becoming whole?* he wondered. His eyelids grew heavy, and he drifted into a most blissful sleep near the pillar.

Chapter Three

Vulnerability

The next morning, Abu was jolted up. The sky was full of thunder. Huge drops of rain were falling. He ran down under the cover of a rock formation. His clothing and belongings had gotten drenched. The rain was relentless, and the whistling winds had turned from hot to cold. Each hour he grew more uncomfortable. He wanted to continue his journey, but the storm persisted. The day gave way to night, and the night to dawn.

This continued for a few days. Abu felt frustrated, and yet, he kept remembering the teachings of patience. This was an opportune time to exercise and breathe into the discomfort. He was trying.

Finally, at one daybreak, the storm had passed. By now, though, Abu felt weak and unwell. He was sneezing and coughing and felt a chill. His body ached. He had not slept well for days and had had little food. He suddenly felt alone and vulnerable, so different than he had felt just several days prior. He missed the comfort of his home, bed, and family. He looked around. There was no one in sight. He knew he had to get up and continue his journey. With effort, he slowly made his way back to the dirt trail, taking him through the woods. He had to lean on his walking stick. He kept looking for a person or animal. *Any sign of life would be nice*, he thought. He felt raw and alone.

He kept thinking of faith and patience. He closed his eyes and saw the stars wrap around him. He recalled how the ants never gave up. He thought of the exercises and meditations he had learned from the teachings. He remembered the stories. And yet, Abu felt depleted, sad, and scared. Tears began to roll down his face.

How can it be? he thought. *Are we this weak and fragile?*

The hours of the day were lending themselves now to dusk. He was not looking forward to being alone, but he had to take his rest. Suddenly, from afar, he saw a beautiful deer. She was so pure. Magical. Vulnerable.

He got closer. He saw a herd of deer dancing around an elegant glass pillar. It appeared to be rooted into the earth. There was an undeniable sense of solidity that belied its fragile beauty. The scene was spellbinding.

Abu walked up to the deer.

"Salam," he said.

She nodded her head, her doe eyes looking into his.

"I've been feeling ill and alone and have been traveling for days. I thought I would never find another pillar!" Abu said, as he began to get choked up, tears brimming in his eyes.

The deer lovingly stepped over to him and said, "Oh, I'm so sorry. You must be exhausted. Why don't you rest with us tonight?"

"Yes," he replied. "Thank you. I would really love that." He felt touched by her kindness and gentle demeanor, and it was so good to talk to someone.

He continued, "I'm sorry, but can you please tell me what pillar this is?"

The deer looked into his eyes and gently said, "Vulnerability."

"Aahhh," Abu said with a nod of his head. *Vulnerability*, he thought. *Of course ...*

The deer nestled in close and, comforted by their presence, Abu heard the teachings from *The 11 Pillars*.

THE TEACHINGS

"The wound is where the Light enters you."
Rumi

It had all caught up with me. After a harrowing two-year period of steady stress and disappointment, I was finally depleted. I found myself struggling with performing basic daily tasks and coping with simple obstacles. My heart felt raw. I heard and saw everything in a way that was magnified times ten, and it was having a profound effect on me.

The blaring TV bothered my ears, and the everyday sounds of LA traffic overwhelmed my sensory system. Seeing a homeless person broke my heart, and I would cry at a commercial. I was experiencing deeper levels of discomfort with my feelings as each day progressed and it did not go away. I thought it would last a few days, but it was now a month. I felt so vulnerable.

Still, I persevered, allowing myself to discover what my spirit wanted me to acknowledge. Soon, the message was clear: I needed to take a pause and allow this "unraveling" to continue of its own accord. I needed to lighten up my schedule and embrace whatever feelings bubbled up to the surface. I needed to let the tears flow and finally process the avalanche of emotions that had been restrained from expression by the fast pace I had attempted to maintain.

I also needed to tune in to what my spirit yearned for each day—to sit in quiet, in prayer, or in nature; to read the books of philosophy, poetry, and spirituality; to hear the sounds of Vivaldi, the native bamboo flute, or the

Indian ragas. The more I tuned in, the more I desired these "soul gifts," as my spirit was drinking them all like a healing potion.

In time, I began to understand where and what needed to heal. I focused on the wound—the space of shattered dreams and broken promises—and caressed it, honored it, and slowly came to peace with it. As I began to reconnect with the whisper of my soul, my heart broke open wider, and I had an awakening ... a realization of myself, the Universe, and a deeper understanding of all Its makings. Suddenly, I felt I had opened up to a new world, a vastness of being, and at the center of it was my heart, shining ever so brightly.

Vulnerability is a key pillar to spiritual enlightenment. It is the opening of the heart to its purest essence, where we can better see and understand the suffering of ourselves, as well as others. This enables us to both find healing and become healers: two essential components on our journey to self-realization. And it is in this awareness that we are led to our inner light and our purest essence. Vulnerability is the sacred portal to the Maker: a holy pilgrimage for our soul.

But this sacred pilgrimage can also be challenging, because we must swim beyond the shallow waters and find our way into the deeper terrains of emotion. This can make things feel more raw, heightened, even naked. In this nakedness of being, our feelings and senses are more intensified. We may feel uneasy. We may also feel lost, hurt, or confused until we find our way through the twists and turns, and the healings and awakenings, that vulnerability presents to us.

In this chapter, we will explore the many complex sides of vulnerability and better understand why it is truly one of the greatest gifts we have been given.

The Misguided Myths

The expression of vulnerability hasn't truly been embraced in our culture. We may have been called "crybabies" as children, or told to "stop crying," as if it were something to be ashamed of. Men have often been told that they weren't supposed to cry because it was a sign of weakness. And, in cultures like mine, women were told to hide their emotions and simply "bear it."

In addition, it seems that in modern culture we always have to be "on" and say we're "doing great," even if this is not the case. Truth is, it is scary for most of us to bear our soul, for we also fear being shunned, or judged. We have an old saying in Iran that speaks of how when we are happy, good friends are all around us, but when we're down and depressed, many of those same friends disappear.

For these reasons and more, it's no wonder that we find it so easy to shut off from the world, to not be open to deep love or the pain of growth, and to distance ourselves from it all. But this is a disservice to ourselves, to one another, and to our world. When we distance ourselves or hide our true emotions, we think this is strength. But actually, this is merely a popular illusion of strength. Real strength is embracing our vulnerability and saying, *I know that the road may be winding and I may fall, but I know it will lead me to an oasis.* This is strength; this is courage; the allowance and embracing of vulnerability.

So, you see, contrary to popular belief, our biggest strength is our vulnerability. It is how we can best honor our mission, serve our world, and strengthen our faith. Strength is about that which builds us up to become more whole. And as an evolving society, my hope is that we get to a point where, when we see someone crying, instead of asking, *"What is wrong with you?"* we might ask instead, *"What is awakening inside of you?"*

Transformations

Imagine a caterpillar. He wants and desires to become a butterfly. That is his journey, his purpose, in this life. And once he transforms, he will fly and explore, drinking of the sweetness and fragrance of all that is. Butterflies beautify nature and inspire us, because in their vulnerability as a caterpillar, they awaken to who they truly are. And yet, they have to go through the process of transformation that starts with vulnerability, as a worm: slow-moving, vulnerable to attacks, fully subjected to the elements until, at last, they are free.

Similarly, a bird knows there are dangers inherent to flight that make her vulnerable. But to avoid these risks would mean denying her most authentic expression—that which allows her to survive and thrive in the world. This vulnerability allows the exploration of self-realization, because to assume the open position of flight, you have to open yourself up to danger. Conversely, a clam stays in her shell, experiencing less chance of danger, but a greater likelihood of stagnation.

There is much we can learn from observing nature. Now, let's look at some common scenarios in our own lives where vulnerability can lead to transformation.

The Reasons and the Seasons

Why do we become vulnerable? Can it be avoided? Is it necessary for our growth?

Vulnerability can occur at various times and seasons in our lives and for different reasons. I have found that there are two basic approaches we can take when it comes to vulnerability. We can *Allow It In* or *Seek It Out*. Let's look at how each approach might work:

Allow It In

To allow vulnerability in is to embrace it when the heart has awakened to feelings of pain, sadness, betrayal, or grief, or when we feel more raw and depleted in our reserve. Here are a few instances:

Something New

Life changes with work, school, or home can create feelings of vulnerability, because these aspects can represent a radical shift from that which we are comfortable with. College graduates, for example, can feel vulnerable, as they are thrown into a more complex and less predictable world of work and bills after living in a more sheltered college setting. They don't know how they will adjust to new conditions and routines, or how they will feel outside of their safety net. They each have to find their own pace and adjust to this new change of lifestyle and position. In time, they will become comfortable.

Running on Empty

Many experience vulnerability after a long period of feeling pressure, stress, or overwhelm. In time, the stressed-out soul and body become more depleted, until activities slowly and inevitably come to a halt, once you realize that you just cannot push so hard anymore. Some people fight this and continue pushing, which only hastens the inevitable burnout. What is needed at this time is to honor our being, to step back and nurture ourselves until we can slowly ease into healing.

Social Uncertainty

Sometimes unexpected things happen that uproot our entire community, country, or world. Natural disasters like hurricanes, earthquakes, or fires, tragedies centered around mass violence or war, and public or political unrest, are all unsettling or even devastating events that create a sense of immense vulnerability.

And then in 2020 we had the global pandemic of COVID-19, which made each country and person feel vulnerable as lives were radically changed overnight. We all felt that the ground underneath our feet had suddenly shifted, not knowing what lay ahead in the next days or weeks. This vulnerability, although initially difficult, led many to find their deeper truths, and understand better what they truly wished for after the pandemic.

"Emotional" Heart Attacks

Somewhere along our life's journey, we feel other more pronounced types of pain in the form of major disappointments, heartache, betrayal, loss, and sometimes just the realities of life itself. We actually feel this pain in our heart center—our heart chakra—and it can feel like our heart is literally breaking. And just as a heart attack is a warning of our physiology, a "break of the heart" is an attack of our emotional center on our soul, and a turbulent awakening of heightened vulnerability.

Sometimes, it isn't until years after these "heart attacks" that we find the ability to go back to heal or resolve them. It is in this space of rawness that we slowly understand, gain insight, forgive, and find clarity, before coming into new realizations and awareness. Vulnerability is the transition process from pain to acceptance, from confusion to clarity, from fragility to empowerment, from uncertainty to assurance, and from not seeing our inner light to embracing it.

Seek It Out

This is a more proactive form of vulnerability that we consciously implement as part of our desire for self-realization. In addition to the various contemplative and reflective practices, it can often involve "bringing out the skeletons" and confronting aspects of ourselves that are uncomfortable. This process invariably conjures up feelings of exposure and vulnerability. Here are a few examples:

Deep Spiritual Practice

For those who are in spiritual practices and want to become more awakened, there is often a need to delve deeper into the various layers that have been weighing heavy upon their souls, in order to find deeper connection with Source. In a way, we have to first feel lost in order to find ourselves. This requires honesty and openness. Here, through meditation, prayer, mantra work, reflection, reading poetry, listening to soulful music, or spending time in nature, a stirring awakens our heart into feeling more vulnerable, as we come face-to-face with our purist emotions. We go deeply into them to understand, release, and ultimately embrace the lessons and teachings, thus furthering our spiritual evolution and transformation.

Therapy/Self-Help

Those who choose therapy or other self-help practices usually embrace a process of time and discovery, thus uncovering the deep wounds and scars so they may heal. At first, this creates much uneasiness, as the process involves going into their history, stories, and all things buried. Facing the realities of one's self and life is an act of courage, and embracing vulnerability is an act of strength to these seekers. In time, their reward is beyond measure, for through this journey of baring their heart and soul, they experience the gift of healing and become more whole.

Exploring the Big Questions

Vulnerability is not always about painful emotions and heartache. It can also be the result of the soul yearning to open itself to a higher awareness.

In this case, we may come to a point in our evolution where we question our existence, our purpose, and the Universe. In this questioning, we yearn to discover more about who we are, as well as our connection to Source. Our soul's thirst is quenched only by drinking more and more from the various wisdom traditions. In this quest for meaning and insight, we feel the stirrings of our soul asking us to go deeper.

Close to eight months after my mother's earthly departure, I felt a deep yearning to dive into theology and world religions, and just to sit with God. In the previous years, care for my mom had consumed my life. Now, I lengthened my practice daily and so loved my hours of being with the Beloved and all the wisdom teachings of great masters. I would watch nature videos or study cultures who lived in rural settings. The slow pace of their life was a mirror to mine as I felt no rush. I was just enjoying and embracing the moments. And a season after, I felt deep awakenings that so stirred my soul. I had found diamonds in the rust ... water in the desert, quenching my thirst.

The Art and Soul of Vulnerability

Besides coping with difficulties and embracing personal growth, vulnerability is key in the mindful pursuit of our life path. Our work or mission calls the heart to awaken to something that is beyond just the self. We yearn to contribute to the greater good, and this often requires us to embrace vulnerability so that our hearts can "break open" from the purest space within us.

Imagine a memorable painting, piece of music, or poem, and what it might take to create such a great work. Clearly, the artist or composer would need to access the space of an "open heart." In this way, vulnerability serves as a platform for creativity, as this openness enables the artist to "step out on the ledge" and fearlessly manifest their new visions. This is the essence of virtually any form of impactful creative expression.

And yet, the artist is always taking a risk in this creative act, never knowing what might stream into their heart during this open, free-flowing process, or what kind of imprint their new work might leave in their life. And, of course, there is always a risk with how their work will inevitably be received by the public. Such are the challenges we all face, in one way or another, with most any mission-based path we may choose.

Many healers, intuits, and people of faith make it a consistent practice to embrace vulnerability. They have learned to make it their strength, for it enables their hearts to see and feel the various emotions and plights of others. This grants them an uncommon level of empathy and compassion. And it is in embracing this vulnerability that they sit in solitude, communion, and prayer to connect deeper to Source and remain receptive and open. This openness guides them to become better teachers and healers.

This vulnerability can also bring about an unusual degree of strength and courage in the master teacher. The prophet Imam Ali always prayed in a quiet space of sacredness, even on his final night when he knew he was in danger. As his enemies plotted to kill him, he allowed himself to remain vulnerable, never deterring from his mission or path.

Exercises for Vulnerability

No matter where you are in your journey, you cannot reach that coveted moment of awakening without first embracing the uncomfortable nature of vulnerability. Here are some exercises and ongoing practices that will support you in this process:

- Give yourself additional time in the morning, afternoon, and evening to do your chores or tasks. Do not overwhelm yourself with the pressure of speed or rigid deadlines. Ease into things.

- Allow your body to rest more each day. Go to bed earlier and, if possible, take a nap during the day.

- Give yourself thirty minutes a day to sit in quiet somewhere that's relaxing and beautiful, like a garden or a park. Spend time in nature, take walks, go near the water, or enjoy a picnic. If you're at home, listen to something healing, such as meditative music, nature sounds (such as waterfall soundscapes), bamboo flute, or Tibetan bowls. Try to empty all thoughts and just be.

- If you want to access this "raw space" within you, listen to music that evokes deep emotion in you. Allow the tears. And if you prefer, journal or just let your body guide you to a creative expression.

- Stay away from situations, devices, or people that may overwhelm or stress you. You can simply tell them you are taking some "me" time.

- Do something you love each day just for you, whether it is going for a walk, listening to music, or cooking.

- Try to meditate each day. Start at five minutes. This will help you embrace silence. Sitting, walking, or candle or object meditation can all support you.

- Don't judge yourself, but rather, be kind to yourself. Remember you are on a sacred pilgrimage.

- Read a book of poetry or on spirituality. This helps open you up to deeper emotions and higher-minded thinking.

- Stay positive; don't give in to despair. Know that vulnerability is an act of courage and strength, and you will be rewarded for your efforts with priceless awakenings. With each tear, you will gain further wisdom.

- When in sacred space, see yourself as a beam of light, as part of the Divine Tapestry. Connect to this and to the sages and masters before you.

One of the most crucial distinctions we can make about vulnerability is that it is an invaluable strength and not a crippling weakness. It is an upward energy surge to the higher self, and to our connection to Source. In opening our hearts, we will see and experience the magical array of colors in this garden of life. For vulnerability is a gift to ourselves … an endless field of possibilities.

ʃ

O Heart …
Your tears are pearls of wisdom,
awakening you,
to the beauty within.
Find faith in this …
for you are woven in love,
and born from Light.
Allow the unraveling …
Trust its journey.
See your beautiful essence,
radiating light and love.
See the miracle …
that is you.
Believe.

ʃ

Abu was listening with all his heart. Tears ran down his cheeks. He understood it now. He needed to go through this. He needed to be uncomfortable, to be raw. He had to trust it and allow it to unfold.

"So, this is my strength, for it is connecting me to a deeper layer within myself?" he asked.

The deer nodded.

Abu sat staring at the night sky and laid down next to all the deer. Finally, after many restless nights, a deep, peace-filled sleep found him.

Chapter Four

Purification

As Abu woke up the next day, he felt as if someone had literally cracked open his insides. He didn't know exactly how to handle this level of vulnerability. The deer had all gone about their day, and he felt exposed. How was he going to get through it? Was he strong enough? What if he got sick again? What if he continued feeling this way? The what-ifs played in his head, and by midday he was even more tired. He really wanted to get up and continue his journey, but his lack of stamina on all levels told him he still needed to rest. He felt so much more at ease when the deer were there in the evening with him, as they brought him much comfort at this uneasy time.

The vulnerability continued each day. He felt there was an ocean in him, at times stormy. He was moved to tears easily. The star had said to *believe*, and that is what he needed to keep reminding himself. So, he held on to the teachings. He could not stop, not now.

And then, the morning came … the morning he knew he had to continue and follow his quest. Slowly, he made it to his feet, leaning on the tall stick.

The vastness ahead continued for days. Abu had lost track of time. The path was not changing, all seemed steady. He did not see any more pillars and was growing tired. He rested in a spot for a few days, regaining his strength. Once again, he got up determined to continue and find the next pillar. Although the terrain was not difficult, the dark night made it hard to see ahead. He fell quite often and cut his knees and elbows. The cuts were burning. He knew he would have to tend to them soon. This, coupled with the emotional fragility he was feeling, was challenging him. But he continued.

By the time he stopped again, the blue velvet sky had filled up with stars. He felt comforted by this, knowing their light was guiding him. He was carrying all the teachings within him. He felt supported and strengthened thinking of each of the pillars he had encountered thus far.

After what seemed like weeks, the terrain was changing again. There were more trees and rougher roads. The next day he fell again, this time tumbling down and landing hard on his behind near a river. His knee was bleeding from the fall, and his back had taken a beating.

He quickly put his hands in the cold water to get relief from the stinging. He immediately took his clothes off and went into the river, splashing water on his wounds. This was a welcome change for his tired body and soul.

The river was flowing beautifully into a small cascading waterfall. He went and sat underneath it. He felt a deep healing enter his body, as the cool water was calming the burns. Fatigued from all the falls and weeks of travel, it seemed to permeate his physical, mental, and emotional self. He was drinking of this blessed feeling. It was exactly what his soul was craving.

Abu sat staring at the waterfall. It was so soothing, like a lullaby. He noticed the water was standing tall, as a pillar. *Is this a pillar?* he whispered to himself.

He heard a chorus of melodic voices amidst the waters. "Yes."

Startled, he looked around. The waters seemed as if they were humming.

Softly, he asked, "What pillar is this?"

"Purification," sang the answer in a sweet melody.

Purification, he thought. He was intrigued.

He sat quietly, as the waters soon began to sing the teachings of *The 11 Pillars*. He was so ready to receive this gift.

THE TEACHINGS

"Solitude is the place of purification and transformation,
the place of the great struggle and the great encounter."
Henri Nouwen

"I can't seem to go deep within," she said. "It's as if I'm blocked and unable to connect to my own soul. How can I create purification if I can't even get in?"

She would try her best and diligently take notes in all the workshops, but I knew she could not understand why she could not create healing, release, and purification. She was not ready: her intention was not from her heart, but rather strictly from her head. She felt logically this was what she should do, but she was not ready emotionally or spiritually to look inside.

A year later, after going through a separation and divorce, she felt broken and fell to her knees. And in those moments of vulnerability, she delved into her soul and swam effortlessly through the tides. Every molecule within her wanted to heal, so her intention came from the purest place. She dedicated a year of her life to purification and healing, as her heart and head awakened to this. She transformed as this process unfolded, and the Rumi books she had not understood—and the various teachings she had not grasped—were now revealing themselves like stars in the night sky. She had embraced this purification, and in this allowance—along with therapy, meditation, and prayer—she found herself.

To purify is to go to the purest place within the soul—where our truth is not jaded or tarnished—and release, create acceptance, forgive, heal and, essentially, cleanse: to "extricate the debris" so we may re-emerge whole again. This is seldom easy to navigate. It requires allowance, intention, and accountability to delve into the world within, where we uncover and de-layer our baggage, see our pain, and thus, create healing.

Yet, this purification process is critical because it provides an inner cleanse of the accumulated residue, so that we may continue to evolve and grow. And while it is not a onetime process, the first time we truly experience purification is often the hardest, for it is new to us and requires much time, patience, honesty, accountability, and allowance. Like riding a bike or learning how to swim, it can initially feel scary and uncertain. But as we continue to embrace purification, we can breathe through it and navigate the process more easily over time.

The journey of life entails many hills and valleys. There is joy, there is pain, and there is triumph and suffering. For the spiritual soldier, suffering is often a gateway to the path of purification and healing. It is through the cracks of the dark corridors of our being that the light can be seen. And it is there that pearls of wisdom replace the tears of our pain, and we find our guidance on this path.

Very few souls, if any, have come into this world with such a high level of awareness that they do not have to purify. Even most sages and prophets go through this process of inner cleansing, and even suffering, to find a more pure and absolute connection to God and their inner light.

In Sufism, this asceticism is called "riazat," and it is regarded as an important part of the practice to the path of enlightenment. For it is through such suffering that we usually choose to go deeper. And it is in those deeper realms that we confront our pain, scars, and flaws as humans. Only then may we find forgiveness, acceptance and, ultimately, our healing, as we slowly begin to understand the Ways of the Universe and gain more insight, wisdom, and connectivity.

Moses had to go through the desert for forty days without food or water. And it was through this riazat, which brought him to his knees, that he found his purification, thus making him more accountable to his mission.

During a period of my life where I was yearning more and more for spiritual awareness and enlightenment, I found myself needing to rest after a medical procedure that had appeared out of the blue. The procedure was simple, but the delays for it had depleted my reserve and, so, my healing process took longer. During those weeks of needing to exercise so much patience, I found myself becoming more empty of residue, and discovered deep perspectives and pearls of wisdom. At the end of my healing, I felt my riazat had raised my spiritual and emotional antennas to a new level. Such is what riazat does. The suffering forces you to sit, observe and, hopefully, confront, purify, and find new wisdom.

Allowance

Allowance is about giving way to something and "allowing" its energy to be what it is intended to be. In allowance, we are saying, *I will not block it, but rather, open the gates to it.*

This is something I've practiced through the years that has so helped me heal: I allow tears. I allow pain. I allow grief. And I allow and trust the process. When someone says, *When are you going to get over this?* I say, *I own my pain*, and that means that I hold on to it until I can let it go.

Over a decade ago, when my father suddenly passed away, I was in shock and grief. After a few months, the grief was less intense, yet I still felt the pain of loss. I remember a few people told me to get over it. My response was that healing takes time: that you cannot get over the heartache of losing someone you have loved for forty-five years in a month or two. The pain lessens and it fades in color, but healing is always a journey of steps. The grief has to set in and play out for the acceptance and eventual release to happen. Only then can the rawness subside.

For purification to find wings in our practice, we need to allow ourselves to be open to all that is involved in the process of self-healing. By simply allowing, we are able to engage the various pathways—to go through the turns, slide through the openings—and reclaim the diamond of our soul, through purification. This process of allowance is essential for our growth and requires work. We assume that with age we will create healing and wisdom as we find awakening. However, there are many elderly people who still have not awakened to their inner light. This is why, in addition to allowance, this level of healing needs our intention.

The Intention Behind Our Wings

To want or desire something is not exactly the same as intention. Intention has to have a strong wind behind it to manifest. In all my years of private practice, I have encountered many who have stated that they intend to create change or healing ... when they can find the time. In my experience, such a time never arrives: we have to create it. Never is everything so aligned that we can carry out our intentions without some effort. In life, there are always many variables. The person whose intention is healing, needs a driving force behind them. For intention by itself is a noble thought, but to be carried out as an action it needs that push, that yearning.

When we do anything in life, we either give it our all or do it half-heartedly, inconsistently. What we intend dictates how much effort we put forth. If our intentions are strong and come from the depth of our being, we give more. If not, it is harder to push through. When our intention is pure, the Universe hears us and the blessings that come our way have a richer resonance. When our intention is impure, we tend to manipulate and play mind games. Even if the outcome is favorable, it is colored by untruths. And then somewhere in our journey, we have to answer karmically for this.

During a period of my life when I worked with a lot of high-profile people, I recognized how some tried to befriend me to see if they could access my "contacts." They were not interested in me, but through me they were hoping to get to a Miss or Mr. X. Their intentions were jaded, and I could see right through it. (This is the huge benefit of a life of meditation and constant inner work: the impurities are very clear!) Now, we all have done this in varying degrees and circumstances. But as we get wiser, it becomes more apparent to us when we are sitting in the purity of the soul, and when we are not. We know when we are being manipulative and when we are not. When coming from the place of light and truth within us, intention carries a beautiful resonance in our experience and drives us to a higher plateau of awareness and wisdom.

The Accountability Factor

When we want to create purification, we need to be held accountable, not necessarily for our mistakes or shortcomings, but for our healing. No one else can do this for us. Being accountable is, in essence, being responsible for our own actions, thoughts, and words. It is also about being truthful to ourselves about what needs to be healed. This requires us to see our patterns and actions, and then to own them, and that is one of the most critical things needed for the process of purification and healing.

I know a woman who blames others for everything. She sees herself as the forever victim, righteous and perfect, but fails to be accountable for her own actions. When she hurts others, she is too afraid to look in the mirror. So, her cycles continue and, at fifty, she is still spiraling and not able to heal.

Healing is hard work, not unlike a "real job." You have to show up and do the tasks at hand, day in and day out, until you feel the weight is being lifted. There are no shortcuts or gimmicks. This is why many people get even more frustrated when they go to therapy. It's real work! Some wind up blaming the therapist and dropping out. In truth, it takes time to untangle the web created, and forgive, allow, and intend, until those deep scars begin to lighten.

The Process of Healing

Healing is a process that, first and foremost, requires our courage and accountability. Healing is not about denying a wound, but helping the wound to be sealed. When we hurt or are in pain, the wound is still fresh, even if years have gone by. It is like an open wound that keeps bleeding from time to time, for it has never been mended.

A dear student of mine had a breakup with her boyfriend of many years. She thought she would marry this man. After the breakup, she suffered for a long while with bouts of sadness and depression lasting for months that became years. Clearly, a part of her did not want to believe the breakup had happened at all. She kept living in the past, absorbed in the memories she shared with him.

Eventually, she got tired of hanging on to the pain and committed herself to therapy and self-work. It was then that she allowed herself to see the full scope of the relationship and accept her own accountability in the situation. She then brought forth a powerful intention to move forward and start a new chapter in her life, as she wanted to find a partner and fall in love.

Once this intention became clear, she allowed herself to go deep and create purification, as she emptied herself of the resentment, hurt, and anger. It took time, but like a warrior, she battled with her insecurities and pain, and slowly walked into acceptance and healing. Like a wilted flower, she found new life under the rays of self-love and forgiveness, and bloomed beautifully once again. And finally, she freed herself and the wound was healed. In time, she met another man, fell in love, and has now been happily married for ten years.

Healing does not always imply that a wound will completely disappear, for we may never fully recover from certain experiences. However, these experiences will never hurt us as they once did, once healing takes place.

The Passage of Time

Healing is not always about forgetting the pain, or having it disappear, but rather it is about an acceptance of the pain, and finding a way to move away from it and continue in a healthy pattern. In many instances, a passage of time is needed to own it, mourn it, forgive it, and then either release it or accept it, in order to continue and move forward.

A woman lost her beloved brother in a plane crash. He was her everything, and the trauma she experienced was so severe that her physical and psychological state had become deeply compromised. Every time she spoke of the incident there was always a pause, and her voice would crack for a few seconds at the remembrance. She felt she could never continue her life with any level of normalcy.

Through the years, she would always say that she needed more time to accept the reality, and to mourn it. Both she had been given. But could she ever *completely* heal from that trauma? Maybe not. Did she eventually heal to the extent that she recovered her equilibrium, and was able to move forward with her life and live it fully? Yes. After many seasons, she learned to carry the grief, but not let it own her.

Healing is a journey of steps we take one day at a time. With love and patience, we step into our wound center and allow it to find its way to a form of recovery.

Purification cannot happen without healing, and as we have covered in this chapter, it requires intention, allowance, and accountability. All of these attributes are as interconnected as we are. And just as our eyes connect us to color and beauty, our nose to smell, and our mouth to taste, the interconnection of these attributes gives us the full experience of purification.

This pillar is so critical to our well-being, for without purification, we are fragmented, like a broken vase. But with it, the diamond emerges, brilliant, radiant, and full of warmth.

Exercises for Purification

- Do a meditation and visualize yourself on the dirt near a riverbank. As you sit there, see what emotions or experiences come up that you want to give to the river to carry away from you. Envision this, and bless each one as it is carried away.

- Think of a subject that has pained you, then write down the emotions that come up. Consider each emotion one at a time: breathe it in, feel it, own it, then release it through your exhalation, giving it to the winds to carry. Try elongating the inhalation and exhalation each time.

- Go on a journey of inner reflection in your meditations and allow yourself to see your inner wounds. Now imagine a warm, golden-red light focusing on your wound and visualize it healing.

- Write down the experiences you feel you have not gotten over, and that upset your equilibrium. Then, write down your intentions for your life. The space between the experiences and the intentions is where the healing needs to take place. Explore what is blocking you and write down what surfaces. Now, use some of the tools below to help heal each blockage.

Tools to Create Purification and Healing

- ***Breath***: Do "breaths of fire" as you think of an experience that has scarred you, releasing the anger and hurt through the breath. See examples of Breath of Fire on any online video platform.

- ***Nature***: Walk in nature, hug a tree, feel the love from nature embracing you. Put your hands and feet into the soil. Feel the coolness and healing of Mother Earth.

- ***Journaling***: Journal regularly, then go back and re-read your journals. Writing your emotions on paper helps you process them more effectively.

- ***Self-Reflection***: Write down areas of your life where you feel you can better yourself, and then set a plan in motion.

- ***Prayer***: Engage in prayer and communion, and in this allowance of sacred connection, create purification and healing.

- ***Earth and Water Therapy***: Put your hands and feet in the earth or water to neutralize your energy field.

- ***Sound or Word Therapy***: Use reading, or listening to sound waves or music, as a channel to go deep within. See what will unfold within.

- ***Poetry/Spiritual Wisdom Books***: Words are powerful, and a great conduit for our healing and getting in touch with deeper emotions.

- ***Burning Letter Ritual***: Write a letter to whatever or whomever has pained you, that you are holding on to. After you write it, fold it, and burn it. As it burns, bless it away for the lessons it taught you.

- ***Other examples***: Fasting for spiritual reasons, enduring long periods of silence, or abstaining from certain earthly pleasures.

In purifying our being, we are not only creating healing, but we are learning from the lessons, evolving, and finding a deeper space of peace within us. From this space, the wilted flowers will blossom again, and the garden will be revived full of promise and hope.

❦

O Beloved …
I sit at the door of healing.
I have carried pain and tears …
heavy they have been upon my soul.
I am ready now …
to give them to the wind and the rain,
to the rivers and the streams
to carry away …
May I see the lessons,
may I hear the whispers,
and may I find myself whole,
once again.
And through this,
may I walk into a new day of healing,
of acceptance,
of renewal.

Abu felt every word of the teachings. He felt his body and soul so needed to hear these. He drank of each word. It was quenching his inner thirst. Just being near the water, he felt more purified, in a sense. He had many questions, but then, he knew by now, that the pillar was not going to give him the answers: they had to come from within him. He was getting the teachings and the guidance, but the work was up to him. This he had gathered from his journey.

Chapter Five

Love

Abu spent weeks near the water. He had lost all sense of time and was basking in the teachings. This allowed his soul to sit in this sacred reverence. At times, he felt challenged. He was not sure if he could understand everything. Yet patience now came with less of a struggle, as he so yearned for the deeper connections. He knew this would take time.

He was vulnerable still. His heart held many emotions. Being on this journey of self-realization had opened him up to a world he had not seen or known before. But after the teachings on purification, he knew he had to allow the emotions and thoughts to flow. He felt an energy working through him, guiding him to create deep healing. It seemed he was understanding so much more about life, himself, and the Universe. These were jewels upon his being, brilliant and radiant.

It was hard for him to leave the waters, no matter how long he had been there. It seemed his soul still wanted the healing, the renewal. He patiently allowed it. Early one morning, as he awakened, he knew it was time to move on to the next leg of his journey. His healing would continue. It was flowing, and he would carry it with him into the next step.

Once underway, the terrain was starting to change again. The trail was curvaceous, full of turns, hills, and valleys. He started feeling more rejuvenated with each passing day. He trusted the road and knew that, when it was time, the next pillar would appear.

One afternoon along the way, he heard a whimpering noise and looked around. *What was that?* he wondered. It sounded like an injured dog. He heard it again. Suddenly, he saw the dog. His leg was bleeding. Abu leaped into the bushes where the dog was.

"You poor baby," said Abu. "Hang on, I will help you."

Quickly, he took out a shirt from his backpack and tore off a part of it. He applied pressure to the leg where the wound was to stop the bleeding. He was successful.

He then wrapped the dog's leg so it would heal better.

Abu patted him on the head. "You are all better now," he said, smiling lovingly at the dog. "I think you'll be all good real soon."

The dog got up, limping, and started licking Abu's face. Abu started laughing.

What an affectionate being this dog is! he thought to himself. *He is so full of love!*

After he saw the dog was better, he said, "Go on now. I am sure your pack is looking for you."

The dog looked at him. He understood. He ran with a slight limp into the woods. Abu watched him run, and felt really good that he had been able to help him.

Abu continued into the heart of the vastness. It held a simple beauty. He could hear the various sounds of nature, the light breeze, the whistle of the leaves on the trees, the choir of crickets. He couldn't see a pillar, but he trusted he would find it when it was time.

The afternoon sun was dimming. From afar on the hill, he saw a figure. He walked closer. It was the dog! The dog started running, but kept looking back at Abu. *He wants to show me something*, Abu thought. He ran to where the dog was headed, to the top of the hill.

There, he saw them: an army of dogs standing at various points on the hill. He had never seen such a sight! The dog he had helped came close to him.

"Is this a gathering?" he asked the dog.

"It's a pillar," said the dog.

"What pillar is this?" asked Abu, not having a clue.

"This is the Pillar of Love," said the dog, wagging his tail with excitement.

"Oh, my gosh, how could I have missed this? Of course! Love."

Abu stood there, as tears came to his eyes. This one, he knew, was at the heart of it all.

Abu sat at one of the points of the hill as the dog recited the teachings from *The 11 Pillars* with enthusiasm.

THE TEACHINGS

> "The best and most beautiful things in the world cannot be
> seen or even touched—they must be felt with the heart."
> Helen Keller

One of my beloved students was struggling with her children and life partner. Her daughter was facing her demons and acting out through doing drugs and displaying erratic behavior. Her life partner was having a midlife crisis, and she felt as if her family was falling apart.

The situation worsened, and finally reached a point of crisis: Her daughter was suddenly going in and out of various rehab facilities, while her partner failed to be present for the family during this difficult period. My student found herself to be playing the role of both punching bag and caregiver, and now, she was truly depleted. She didn't know if her daughter would survive, or if the nearly twenty-five-year relationship with her partner would, either.

However, just when all hope began to dim, she delved deeper into her spiritual practice, to strengthen herself. She increased her prayers, her daily mantra, and her work of service. She was exhausted, but determined to create healing, as her spirit found a new form of empowerment—that which comes from deep, pure love. Through much inner work, she forgave her daughter and her partner for the years of heartache and mental and emotional depletion. She also made it clear to each of them that, while she loved them, they both needed to do some work for themselves and hold accountability for the family unit, and that she needed to love herself as much as she loved them, so that she could find her way.

At first, they did not hear her. But as they saw that she was serious about creating a life for herself, they got it, and the "light bulb" turned on. They both committed to intense therapy work. And for this, she was present and supportive, but not overly involved, for she knew it was a personal journey they each needed to see through. She understood that, to truly love them, she would have to let them do this on their own and find their healing. And this she did.

Today, the unit stands strong. Their love is deep, and their commitment to one another, and to their own well-being, is cemented. As each person found their healing and voice through the pile of rummage they were carrying, the diamond of their soul emerged. And once they accepted their healing, all that remained was love.

When I saw her after, she was beaming and said, "I never stopped loving them, but I had to love myself and let them learn to love themselves."

A true act of love.

Love is the gateway to all the goodness we see and experience in this life. In love, we see the placement of this physical world in a new light, as we find a deeper connection to the Realm Beyond and see one another with more openness, acceptance, and understanding.

Love is all-encompassing and rooted in a God-like quality and essence. If we believe in the goodness of the Universe, or the benevolence of what we call God or the Great Unseen, then we can also believe that all forms of Creation have been created with love, from the plants and trees, and the moon and stars, to our very being. After all, we just need to see the immense wonder and beauty that is before us each day, to understand all is birthed from love.

Love is the common thread that weaves us all together on this long thread of Existence. Once we truly grasp this concept at our core, then we will see the magic of the heart center, of each other, and of this amazing gift which reverberates through our being in each beat of the heart. Nothing is as miraculous, fulfilling, or complete. Such is love, the portal to the ultimate human experience.

Love is also the basis of all spiritual thought and philosophy. It is the root of our tree of life, and it is what's birthed into our being from the time we were conceived. And in truth, it is *us*: we are created from Love and, in essence, we are love itself. It is through love that we find ourself, find God, find goodness, and find joy and peace. It is the connector to all; it is the most magical part of being alive. It is a pillar that, once cemented, will never allow the inner fortress to collapse.

From the time we acknowledge our being, we feel love and understand it at our deepest core. We are born from this love, in our mother's arms, as she carried us in her heart. The heart center identifies beautifully with love, for it is the portal where we experience the radiance of light as it caresses and warms our heart, and makes us feel whole. Love is what makes this crazy life sustainable. Without love, we would have a very hard time finding meaning in our life. Without love, as a flower without water, we would wilt.

In life, many who are open to love honor and allow it, and then treasure and cherish it. They understand that each time they are gifted with it, it is a blessing. But there are many who may fear loving, for that means they have to open their hearts and allow vulnerability, and that is difficult for them. One reason they may not be open to love is because they have been hurt and do not trust it. Another reason is that it poses a challenge to them, for on some level they have never learned about, or felt worthy of, self-love.

Self-love

To some, the notion of self-love may seem absurd. When I asked an elderly woman if she loved herself, she looked at me as if I had said something sacrilegious. She really could not grasp this concept. When I broke it down to her and asked her if she believed she was worthy, if she liked herself, or if she treated herself with kindness, she replied with, "We never thought of any of these things in our time; we were busy raising families and being responsible!"

Well, I thought, *one of the most responsible things we can learn on our journey of self-realization is to treat ourself with love and see ourself as precious beings.* To uphold this is a huge responsibility that will help us to embrace love and kindness, and to honor ourself and each other. Self-love is also a gateway to self-assurance and confidence for the soul, for when we see our own godliness, we will believe in ourself, and thus stand taller and stronger in who we are.

Without self-love, it is hard to truly understand the scope of the Divine within our inner realm. Self-love is actually what helps us connect to the inner divinity: the light within us. As we see ourself as this light—as a sparkle that is beyond precious—we will see our entire world as this light. In loving ourself as God loves us, we will then see all the children of God through the eyes of love; we see our connectivity and our bond of being, made of the same cloth. We will also see nature and animals through this lens of love.

Through our self-love, we see the entire picture of "being" so much more clearly. For when we see ourself as love—as part of the Divine or Universal makeup—and recognize that our existence in this world has been created out of love, then self-love leads to the greater love for all humanity. And it is through this love that we find our heart center's vastness.

Kindness, Compassion, and Empathy

As magical as love is, it is in the sub-pillar of kindness that we get a glimpse of the best part of our humanity. As a people, we are here for a few reasons: to learn, to find joy, and to be of service. We are also here to understand that it is in being kind to ourself and others that we can truly understand the concept of love, for love is most easily channeled through the beautiful platform of kindness.

Kindness is innate to the heart, part of the fabric of our being. It is not an added fabric that we acquire, but one that each human is born with. When we have awakened to this, then kindness is the natural progression for all of our actions and expressions. Equally, to be kind to ourself means to see ourself through the Eyes of God and become a loving parent to ourself. But it is quite simple: kindness *is* godliness.

Kindness is not an act that we engage in once in a while. It is not enough to do an act of charity a few times a year and feel that we did our part for the whole year. Instead, we need to *become one* with kindness, as with our breath, through generosity, understanding, and extending our hearts to one another. When we understand this, then we automatically enter the gateways of empathy and compassion: two of the highest forms of connectivity with one another.

In the sub-pillars of empathy and compassion, we understand the plight of being human, and are aware of the pain and struggle of others. Without empathy and compassion, we would become self-centered people who are not concerned with others. We would not access our goodness, and not live in the humility of the self, but rather, reside in the house of ego and possibly even narcissism.

Sometimes, people feel being empathetic makes them a sponge for the emotions of others. As a sensitive, when I was young I could feel the pain of others, and at times this made me suffer. But as I matured, I learned that to be empathetic does not mean we allow transference of pain, but rather the *understanding* of it. Once we understand another's pain—rather than internalizing it—it births in us the seed of a deeper connectivity, of brother and sisterhood, of humanity and oneness.

Compassion is similar to empathy in that it is also birthed from an understanding: the human understanding of any type of struggle. To be compassionate means to be open in our hearts to the causes, issues, and daily struggles and suffering of all life. Compassion is not about the self, but rather, it is selfless: void of all selfishness.

In Eastern spiritual thought, there is a word called *maniat*, the direct translation of which is "me-ness." When one's soul resides in maniat, they only see me, me, me. It is very important to see the plight of others, and not reside in narcissism or me-ness.

Empathy and compassion awaken the soul to its most humble state. The humility of recognizing the experiences of being human, and the hills and valleys of this journey of life, is what allows us to see through the window of our soul and connects us to the most profound essence of existence— our oneness.

Forgiveness

Forgiveness is a weighty word. And yet, in its allowance and practice, the weight drops off and becomes light as a feather, drifting into the winds of time.

Forgiveness is about two important areas in our life: forgiving ourself and forgiving "all else," which includes other people, and the hand of fate. These both require self-love and accountability, the release of expectation and ego, and not holding any other entity or person responsible for our own well-being. To gift ourself and others forgiveness is one of the highest forms of giving, for it is about recognizing the light and divinity in each one of us, even as we sway with our imperfections.

In life, we all get hurt and, without always knowing it, we inflict pain onto others. That is part of the process of living, learning, maturing, and finding wisdom. To give ourself the permission to put down this burden and its references in our life, means that we have to say to ourself, "I love you, I honor you, and I want to set you free." Forgiving ourself means we have to stop punishing ourself, for punishing ourself does not serve us, but rather, mentally torments us.

Forgiving Self

Many times, we are the harsh judge of ourself, and not the loving parent. We don't nurture our being, and by not seeing that as humans we are flawed, we create more suffering for ourself. Yes, we make mistakes: we make judgment calls that are not always aligned in truth and goodness. To acknowledge this and be accountable for it is commendable. But, to continue to beat ourself up over it is like kicking someone when they are down. How can a person who cannot get up find the strength within to heal? It is not possible.

In order for us to be healed through self-forgiveness, it is critical for us to understand that, when we inflict pain on another, it is because we have not learned to love and honor ourself. The ego is a false shield, a barrier between ourself and others. It is a wall that we have created, most of the time unknowingly. However, it is important to remember that holding on to guilt and self-blame over time does not create healing, nor does it "teach us lessons." Instead, it slowly eats at us.

Forgiveness is a journey of steps. Once the guilt, self-blame, anger, and regret slowly lessen, we understand that our flaws are our teachers, and the lessons we learn can help us to become more awakened and, ultimately, more enlightened. As we take steps toward self-love, we slowly forgive ourself and find our own atonement.

Forgiving Others and Our Fate

When we aspire to forgive another, it is not saying that what they did was ok, but rather, that we do not want it to own us, define us, or to become an obsession. In forgiving others, we are basically freeing ourself. This liberation allows us to see things with more objectivity, and to further understand that all relationships require forgiveness. Even mothers and their children, or husbands and wives, will sometimes feel hurt or pain from each other. Forgiveness is key for them to find resolutions to create healing. In AA, one of the key practices is asking for forgiveness from those we have hurt in our past. It is in this act that much ego is released, and that we uphold our accountability and restore our wholeness and healing.

One of the most important channels for forgiveness is forgiving our fate, the hand of life, or Universe—whatever you wish to call it. As an immigrant from a war-torn country, I have seen many who have been angered by their fate, by what life brought forth. Many were driven out of their homes, and out of the arms of their loved ones, with most unable to see them again. Anger, rage, and frustration were some of the common feelings many experienced. *How could they forgive this?*

The Universe is a guide. It is not the actor in this play of life; it is the Silent Producer. But how your life is directed is up to you and other components, such as war, politics, natural disasters, violence, tragedies, people's poor judgment, etc. It is important for us to remember this. When we feel wronged, it is our right to get angry, and to say this was wrong. But through the anger is the gateway to healing, as we say, *I will forgive it*. And although we may assign blame to it, we choose to forgive it and heal, to be free, and to not hold on to this pain.

Is this easy? Not always. But is it possible? Most always, yes.

When I was young, my friends and I met a young man who was essentially a roaming gypsy. We found his free-and-easy lifestyle and light energy fascinating. One day, he told us his backstory: He had lost all members of his family in a devastating earthquake. Not one or two members, but nearly twenty! He said the first couple of years afterward he was angry at God and the Universe. But now, he said he had forgiven it, for he understood that he had to find his peace, and that his loved ones would not want him to live with such anger. In time, he had learned not only to forgive the hand of fate, but he had given himself permission to live fully, to find joy and love.

So, as we see our heart center, as we hear the heartbeat, as we feel awakened to the Divine and the divinity within ourself, we will see the jewels that are brilliant beyond what we could have imagined. These have been given to us so graciously by a benevolent God: Love ... and its companions—kindness, compassion, empathy, and forgiveness, the crown jewels of the Love Pillar.

Key Exercises for Love:

Walk each day, and see the people and nature that is around you. See each being as magical, as part of you, not separate from you.

- When you interact with others, see them as children of God, as your kin.

- Each day as you awaken, tell yourself that you will live in a state of kindness and understanding, no matter what the day brings forth.

- Give of your time and material wealth to others. Do this graciously, without pause, and see the joy in it.

- To exercise forgiveness, start by forgiving something that may have happened to you, or you are upset about. Each day, repeat, "I forgive, to become whole. I forgive … and bless it away to the winds." Do this each day until you feel free of it.

- Write down what you feel responsible or accountable for. See it and recognize it. See the insight and wisdom gained. Then no longer hold on to it. Repeat each day, "I have learned the lesson, and I will allow forgiveness, in letting it go."

- Recognize those each day who you see are struggling. Listen to their stories, and after, ask yourself if there is anything you could do for them. If you cannot, then just bless them with your love and pure intention. Do not hold on to their struggle, but let it help you further open the windows to your heart to deeper human understanding.

- Take part in a charity or cause; see how it fills up your heart with a deeper resonance of compassion.

- Open yourself to loving by visualizing your heart center expanding into a beautiful golden light. Breathe into it, and exhale it to all around you.

It is in love that we see the best of each other, the essence of our being, and our connectivity to each other and the Universe. Love is the portal to a life that will be full of the richest of life experiences, leaving only footsteps of kindness, compassion, and forgiveness in the sands.

∫

O Great Universe!
From Love
I have been created.
And with love
I shall breathe and live.
Kindness will be my way.
And empathy and compassion
will be my life's service.
I will never close my heart to loving,
for I know this is the reason for my breath and life.
To live in this joy ...
To bask in this greatest of blessings ...
And become one with all through love ...
This is the eternal gift.

Abu *heard* the teachings with his heart. They reverberated through each cell of his being. His soul understood it.

Love is the key, he thought, *and where there is love, there is everything.*

Chapter Six

Devotion

Abu felt a joyous peace walk through him. He did not want to leave this Pillar of Love. The heart center was so pivotal. It had opened him to a new world of endless possibilities and colors. He slept all night and dreamt of rainbows. He spent many days embracing all the love he was giving and receiving from the dogs. His heart was filled with this pure, unconditional love.

At the same time, Abu was starting to appreciate the journey from each pillar to the other, and was eager to travel and find the next one. As a diligent student, he reviewed the teachings from each pillar and practiced them continuously. With each growing day, he felt a deeper connection to all that had unfolded on this path to self-realization.

One morning, as he was awakened by a welcoming sun and a gentle breeze, he knew he was ready for the next leg of his journey. He felt more energized than he had been in weeks.

Abu walked for hours under the hot sun. There was no pillar in sight. Had he made a wrong turn somewhere? He had to give it more time than a few hours! He chuckled to himself. *Patience, Abu*, he thought. *You should know this by now!* But again, after a few days, he was starting once again to question it. So, he kept reminding himself of the teachings on trust and faith.

Abu stood and looked beyond. He saw a meadow of golden hay with some trees around it. A rustling sound could be heard as the long strands of hay would sway upward toward the sky and then bend downward again as a bowing reverence. He was mesmerized, lost in another dimension of time and space. He felt as if he was in a magical trance. He could make out words in the rustling. It was as a whispering prayer, a chant. The dimming sun woke him out of the trance-like state.

"What on earth is going on?" he said out loud.

Abu continued to hear voices and wondered if a pillar was close by. It was as if the hay had heard his thoughts.

"You are at the pillar," they said in unison.

"But where is it?" he asked. He looked around for the pillar, and also to see who was talking to him.

"You are sitting on it," the voices said in unison again.

Abu then realized, it was the field of hay that was talking to him!

Chapter Six: Devotion

He gulped, taken aback.

"You are part of the pillar?" he asked.

"We are the pillar itself," the hay replied in oneness.

Still taken aback, he asked, "What pillar is this?"

"Devotion," they chanted.

Speechless, Abu closed his eyes. The chant was vibrating throughout his body. And soon after, he heard the teachings from *The 11 Pillars*.

THE TEACHINGS

"True devotion is for itself: not to desire heaven nor to fear hell."
Rabia Basri

A middle-aged man, who was a teacher by profession, found a new purpose in his life. He had teamed with an organization to build schools for children in impoverished areas in Iran.

Each year, he would work on building the schools in remote areas, often located in very harsh regions. He traveled by car, plane, train, bus, donkey, and even on foot to get there. Sometimes the roads would be closed because of sleet and snow, and he would need to spend the night anywhere he could find. But he would always show up, and for weeks at a time, live in very basic and difficult conditions. He did this with such grace, patience, and joy, and was grateful for each day.

Although he was not a man of financial means, he devoted himself to this process wholeheartedly, never getting a cent for his hard work, as each dime was put toward the school. He was fiercely dedicated to the tasks at hand and would regularly imagine how the end product would change the lives of the children and their families.

After many years, he was still energized by this mission, and became an inspiration to all who worked with him. He was never deterred from his mission, as he built one school at a time, bringing smiles to hundreds of children. And in each encounter, he would say, "God willing," trusting this light-filled mission with faith, discipline, and patience. He had found a calling, and through a great love for it, had made a powerful difference to all who he encountered. Truly, his life was a portrait of devotion.

The spiritual soldier will give of his heart and soul to the journey of self-realization. He loves this holy pilgrimage, for through its colorful turns and stunning gateways, he is entranced by the sweet fragrance of this mystifying search. He becomes one with the Unseen Forces and delves into the newfound answers, visions, and perspectives that lead him to a profound serenity that is pure joy. A delight like no other embraces this dedicated warrior, and there he awakens to a love that is deeper than the earth itself: that of God, humanity, and service. And this is where the dedicated soldier sits in awe, forever committed to the most sublime of all pillars: devotion.

Devotion begins with a yearning, that craving from within to seek the Beloved. It is not through thought that we experience this deep yearning, but through the soul. Devotion is to the soul what hunger is to the stomach: only when it is fed will it be content—until it senses that hunger once again. As a devotee repeatedly drinks from this ocean of vastness, he will yearn for more, for there is no finality in its satiation: true devotion is infinite.

Devotion is about the loving space of sacredness and the higher connection to the Divine, and not necessarily about seeking an outcome. In this way, devotion is chosen by the devotee as an act of love—an act of faith and belief—because the soul longs for it. Devotees gladly devote their time to purifying and bonding deeper connections, and to serving humanity.

Devotion: The Purest Connection to Love

Devotion is a crucial aspect of our relationship with the Divine. A devotee loves nothing more than this communion, sitting with the Maker and losing themself in Its vastness, thus deepening the connection to the inner light on the curvaceous pathway of self-realization. Students of the Light will always express that the best hours of their lives are when they have sat in communion, or graciously carried out an act of service. Devotion is a compelling component of spiritual practice; it is the wine that intoxicates the self into a space that is pure, beautiful, and infinite.

In many religions, there is a time dedicated to prayer each day. In Islam, prayers are done according to sunset and sundown, noon, and other daily patterns of the sun. The practitioner devotes themself to this each day, no matter where they are. This set pattern carries a discipline that anchors and creates peace within. Many from the Buddhist traditions do daily mantras and chants to welcome the energies for the day or night in peace and blessings. And Sufi dancers twirl for long periods of time. They enter a trance, an ecstatic state of being, lost in the arms of the Divine. Just as this can be created through their continuous twirling and letting go of the "self," this can happen in the space of devotion.

We see such sacred practices in many faith religions. This discipline and dedication is the gateway to deeper connection, peace, joy, and fulfillment. Many times, as we connect in prayer or mantra practice, we lose our sense of the self and become one with All. This sublime state is the biggest gift, for we see the Light that we are, and the Light that holds us in this chain of existence.

Is it possible to have devotion to spiritual practice without being a devotee of a guru or discipline?

Of course! There are many branches of religious and spiritual thought. Each of them have their own set of rules and regulations and do's and don'ts. However, devotion is not about what or who we follow, as much as it is about the purest of intentions that lie within the heart. The devotee intends what they will put forth each day, as they give of themself wholeheartedly to this sacred connection.

Ultimately, devotion is about the heart chakra recognizing that to truly be awakened, devotion needs to be practiced on a consistent basis from the purest place within. Without devoting ourselves, we cannot truly come to a deeper understanding of the Divine Realm, the divinity within us, or our connection to one another.

In my *Servants of Love* program, one of my students loved to sit in the lap of the Divine each day. She would devote all activities around this—not vice-versa—and happily spend time each day in the practice of meditation, reading, and prayer. Her devotion to the journey of being a "Servant of Love" was truly remarkable. She found such joy in each sitting, and she expressed that it was the best part of her life. I knew it was her devotion that was feeding her each day, helping in her healing and awakening. For you see, when we devote time to higher connections, we are saying, *I honor this path, I honor my being, I honor all Creation*. Through this honoring, the gates of love, trust, belief, and kindness all open within us, and our lives feel more enriched and whole. In devotion, we "come home" to the light within ourselves.

The Many Dimensions of Devotion

Under this key pillar of devotion, there are several crucial sub-pillars, such as discipline, dedication, and commitment. Together, they are effortlessly interlinked in many ways, and it is difficult to speak of one without mentioning the others. For example, devotion, as a disciplined form of dedication, needs our commitment, but not because we feel obligated. Instead, we commit as a solidifying extension of our search for more meaning and deeper connection.

I recently conducted a training for a group of women who had felt a calling within them. In the first session, I spoke for three hours about the journey of spiritual service and what it entailed. I spoke of the dedication and the discipline that is required to de-layer, to purify, to learn, to create sacred practices, and to sit in silence. These all require discipline and dedication. I am sure they felt overwhelmed, and maybe a few wondered how they could possibly complete this rather arduous journey, thinking that maybe it was beyond their capabilities.

But just as we learn patience with our studies in school, the same is true of devotion and its sub-pillars. We take one step at a time and do not imagine graduation when we are in the seventh grade: we only imagine the next day, or maybe the next week. We stay focused on wherever we happen to be on the journey. And through exercising the craft of discipline, we will experience this adventure with joy and grace.

The School of Discipline

As we begin the process of learning and going to school, we soon understand the core importance of discipline. Discipline is a "forever tool" that affects every aspect of our life. Without discipline, it is rather impossible to improve at a task, excel at anything, or go from one level to another. So, we learn to get better at any task by giving it our time and attention through practice. Soon thereafter, we can perform these tasks better.

This is largely why we are asked by the education system to show discipline in our studies. We are given our various assignments and homework not only to learn, but to understand that, as we are presented with these tasks each day, we are learning to exercise our beings with a new mindset that demands time, focus, and discipline. Those who have taken any type of music, art, or sports activity know that the only way one can get better is to dedicate concentrated time to that discipline. Eventually, they will acquire better skills and knowledge.

But it also gifts us one other big bonus for our life: Discipline allows us to fulfill our tasks in a more timely manner of ease, as it helps us prevent overwhelm. It is a tool to create structure for our daily plan, instill order in the chaos of our mind and heart, and to know that we can complete all of the various tasks at hand if we give each one the proper space of time and attention. So, it is not surprising that, as adults, we need to practice discipline to truly have a life that is centered in self-realization and, of course, devotion.

Discipline is not about forcing anything, but rather, it is about understanding that to get better at something—to truly grasp it and learn it—we need to be diligent about engaging in it regularly. This is why discipline in spiritual practice is key, for without it, the dough will never rise. Each day, we need to exercise those soul muscles, tone up our mind, awaken our heart, and sit at the altar of learning, in order to grasp this "new code of self-actualization."

Can discipline create rigidity and stifle creativity?

Some have given the word "discipline" a bad rap. Many think that discipline can be detrimental to the creative process. This cannot be further from the truth. When I was working on my first book, *Miraculous Silence,* in the final months before publication, I disciplined myself to show up and devote hours each day to going over the chapters and prayers with my editors. This showing up daily was not only helping me accomplish the task of finishing the book, but in the space of opening up my schedule to do this work, my creativity was blossoming!

Discipline actually helps and supports the craft of becoming more skilled in our creativity, for it teaches us patience, diligence, perseverance, and responsibility. Discipline helps us honor the connection to our craft—or whatever the component happens to be—and is the key ingredient that allows the student to become the teacher, and the teacher to become the master. And through discipline, we flow and connect beautifully to the sub-pillar of dedication.

The Gift of Dedication

I've spoken often about my dedication to the discipline of self-realization. I've described my personal journey of sitting at the Altar of the Divine each day, at my sacred time of 11:00 p.m., which was solely dedicated to my inner practice. Over time, this became the most powerful and integral part of my day. I so looked forward to diving into the deeper realms of my being, connecting to the Great Unseen, and unveiling the hidden treasures of my soul. The sacred practice of meditation, mantra, and prayer led me to the corridors of silence where life's mysteries would unfold, as each door opened into another. It awakened me to new visions and insights, and became a delight for my soul to quench this thirst of discovery.

Dedication is one of the most precious gifts we can give ourselves, for as we dedicate our time and energies to self-realization and higher connection, we journey through hills and valleys of the soul that are truly magnificent. As we dedicate ourselves to such meaningful pursuits, we are allowing love to flow in without condition.

The Act of Commitment

As dedication is a gift of the heart, commitment is the promise of the soul to live its goal and purpose through the trials and efforts that are needed to reach the new plateaus of growth and awareness. Without commitment, the soul may sway aimlessly. Therefore, commitment is the honoring of this promise that is between the soul and the Universe.

Many beings have a fear of the word commitment, for they feel it is binding them to something they cannot escape and thus may cause them feelings of angst or even claustrophobia. Yet, when there is no promise—no "shaking of hands"—then we come and go as we please on our spiritual journey. This often means the distractions and excuses will be many, and that our time to get from point A to point B will take drastically longer.

This is why our spiritual evolution will, at times, demand of us that we make such a commitment. Although the Divine Order does not demand us to "seal the deal" or "sign the contract," it will often gently coax us to commit ... for good reason.

Imagine you are given a mantra that needs to be done each day for forty days. In the repetition and structure of this time energy, you will release key blockages and see new dimensions of your inner making, as you feel more anchored and centered. In time, you will walk into a new footing. But all of this requires your dedication and commitment. Without fully committing to the practice for forty days, you will not receive the full benefits of the mantra.

Can this level of commitment make one feel caged?

It depends how you perceive it. I have known many individuals over the years who have had a fear of marriage. I have seen them struggle with this for different reasons, but mostly because the name itself scares them.

One client I knew was so petrified of marriage that, at the age of forty, he thought of running away on the day of his wedding. He had been with his fiancée for many years, but the thought of getting married gave him severe anxiety and made him sweat uncontrollably. The day of the wedding, those closest to him were worried, thinking he would be a no-show. But something interesting happened. He had a choice: to make a commitment and see where this new path might lead to, or run away and destroy the beautiful bond he and his fiancée had already cultivated through their long-term relationship. Fortunately, he chose the first. And the moment he said, "I do," the fear in him disintegrated. He went on to love being a husband, and eventually a father.

If you truly honor yourself, you will honor your growth and want to create a more fulfilling life. This will require your word—the handshake, the commitment—at many points along the way. This word is your promise to honor yourself. When you do this with love, then the commitment is not a cage, but rather a window to a better world inside of you. This is the gift of commitment. It will support you to reach new heights of awakening, as you can more fully embrace this loving pillar of devotion.

A mystic loves devotion more than their own breath: the longing and yearning that streams into a loving prayer, a continuous hymn, or the sweetest of all embraces—the silence of the pathways to the Maker. The deep peace that envelopes our being in the minutes and hours of connection, is an ecstatic song for the heart and food for the soul, as it becomes the channel … the conduit of this stream of higher consciousness and divinity.

Key Exercises for Devotion/Discipline/Dedication/Commitment

- Set aside at least ten minutes each day for meditation or a mantra practice. This will help your mind to invite discipline. If you cannot do this exactly at the same time, set a time close to it. Slowly, you may yearn to increase this time yourself.

- Devote time to daily prayer or reading from spiritual writings/poetry.

- Take at least fifteen minutes per day for absolute silence. This will help you hear the whispers of your soul.

- Dedicate each day to doing something for nature, an animal, or a person that is in need of your care.

- Commit to a specific goal, i.e., exercise and health, learning, meditation, art, etc. Keep a daily or weekly journal of your commitment.

Note: Being of service is another huge channel for the practice of devotion, for it is a selfless act of love. As we devote time and energy to service, we are seeing more clearly—and understanding more deeply—the essence of our Being, and our relationship with the Infinite. (More on that next, as service is its own pillar.)

This key pillar of devotion is not only one of the most sacred, it is one of the most profound in its essence, for it is truly about seeing the Divine in the landscape of our everyday life. To create an inner fortress that will be able to withstand the trials and tribulations of a life well lived, devotion has to be understood, practiced, and honored wholeheartedly.

᭷

O Beloved,
As I find You, I find myself.
As I see You, I see myself.
As I love You, I love myself.
And finally,
I understand ...
That I am free ...
That I am endless ...
That I am a part of You,
and this Divine Tapestry.
I kneel to Your Glory.

᭷

Abu was silent as he took everything in. He knew he was still quite young and maybe could not fully grasp all the teachings. Yet, he understood their value and had always yearned for this connection to the Universe. He sat listening to the chants, losing himself in a feeling of ecstasy, as the deepest of sleeps finally enveloped him.

Chapter Seven

Service

Abu sat with the chants for weeks. He could not get enough of them. He felt a connection that was beyond what he had imagined. He felt as if he was sitting in the Lap of the Divine. The weeks were filled with a stillness that birthed only peace. Finally, one evening, he knew it was time. He was now ready to move on to the next chapter.

The terrain once again was changing. The road was bumpy and there were many twists and turns. He patiently walked with purpose. By mid-afternoon, there were gusts of wind blowing much dust. The winds continued into the night and throughout the days ahead.

One particular day, the winds picked up strength and speed, blowing Abu onto a pile of rocks. He felt a sharp pain and his knee was torn up and bleeding. Barely able to stand, he just sat there, not knowing what to do. Suddenly, he heard a honking type of sound. *Could that be a mule?* Abu wondered. Indeed, it was! He turned to see a mule walking toward him. The mule stopped in front of him and sat down. He was clearly offering to assist. Abu chuckled.

"You are so kind," he said. "Thank you!"

Abu somehow managed to prop himself up on the back of the mule. He felt a mild relief. The mule took him through the trail and stopped at times, so Abu could rest his knee.

"You are pretty amazing," said Abu, as he caressed the mule's neck. "You have not once complained, but have just taken care of me."

The donkey nodded.

After many stops, Abu saw a huge wooden structure from afar. *What is this?* he thought.

The donkey stopped near it, and Abu slowly got off. There was a distinct smell in the air near the structure. Abu looked inside. It was a barn filled with mules!

"What is this?" he asked out loud.

He then heard several voices in unison, as a huge honk: "This is the Pillar of Service."

Abu sat on a bale of hay, stretching his leg out. The *11 Pillars* book was already open to be read.

THE TEACHINGS

"I slept and dreamt that life was joy. I awoke and saw that life was service. I acted and behold, service is joy."
Tagore

I knew a woman who I'll call Caroline. She was an only child, and now that her mother had been diagnosed with cancer and was quite old, she had to take care of her. Caroline resented this disruption to her carefree life, and also felt that her mother did not deserve her attention and kindness, given that she did not have the best relationship with her mom. She did love her mother, but had preferred only seeing her a few times a year for short holiday visits. This would be much different. *Ugh*, she thought, *why does this all have to fall on me?*

When her mother came to stay with her, Caroline was taken aback. She had aged considerably and appeared notably more fragile than the stoic mom she had always known. In the days that followed, she could see her mother did not have the strength to do much for herself, so Caroline began cooking her meals, washing her clothes, and looking after all of her basic needs.

One evening as she bathed her mom, she got a flash of her childhood when her mother used to bathe her. Tears filled her eyes as she had a revelation. She saw and understood the circle of life. She had been the baby decades ago, and her mother had taken care of her. And now, she was taking care of her mom, who was as a child, in need of help. The roles had in a way reversed.

As she continued to care for her mother, she became less self-centered and more loving and forgiving. She realized a deep joy filled her heart each day. In serving her mother, she had awakened to something profound within her: the sacred love, humility, and connectivity of service.

To have a fulfilling life anchored in a deeper inner realization and healing, we need to understand and embrace this key pillar of service. It is when we see another as ourself and want to show up, without conditions, that we find the joy that Tagore speaks of. Service is a "call to action" from the heart as it comes to a deeper understanding and awakening of oneness and our universal connectivity. As we awaken to this, then we further attend to each other and our world.

It is in attending to another that we practice goodness and open our being to becoming more purified. It is in the act of service that we see the face of God and a kinder Universe. Service is not an extra activity or an extension of the self; it is the self—*Itself*—in ultimate godliness, and therefore, a key pillar. It is the way to being a "light carrier." To only be of service once in a while as an act of charity, is to not truly comprehend the significance of service.

Service is not about serving another to earn a brownie point up in the Heavens, but rather, it is about simply engaging in the act of giving: without expecting reward or recognition. I remember a celebrity who always gave quietly to various causes, so no one knew about it. She told me that is how she wished for it to be done, minus any accolades. On the other hand, I knew someone else who would always create huge posts on social media about any act of charity she did. An act of service is about channeling the godliness within us and giving to another—as the Universe has given to us—freely, lovingly, and most importantly, without expectation.

What is quite amazing about this pillar is that as we serve others, we come to a greater understanding and healing within ourselves. In a time of my life when I felt quite stuck and unable to move forward with any major decisions, a wonderful spiritual guide I knew suggested that I focus my attention on serving, so I could get out of my own head. He believed nothing would help me more, and he was quite right. As I focused my energies on serving others, I arrived at new insights about my own situation. I stepped away from just focusing on me and focused more on the "we." I found my own clarity and insights into healing. The experience was rejuvenating and so fulfilling, as the joy of service pumped new hope and life into me.

In my practice of close to four decades, my students and clients knew that I would talk about service as part of their healing process. However, many times I would hear, "Mitra, I am not about service." I would find this statement very disconnected from the human heart. When someone says this, I question what in them has disconnected from the love, joy, and belief in the self. For in giving of the self, we are actually giving back to the self. I also question how or if they know how to "serve" themselves. For when we learn how to serve ourselves, we understand that we need to allow love, give joy, and be good to ourselves, also. And when we know and practice this, we then treat others as we wish to be treated, and thus, understand the deeper connectivity between us.

Service from the Heart

Service does not need to be a big act or make a huge splash. Rather, it just needs to be carried out as devotion, wholeheartedly. Sometimes when we do not serve ourselves and strictly serve others, our energies can get depleted, especially over time, and we can feel resentment and anger. In serving others, we need to also understand we need to serve and give love, time, and attention to our body, mind, and spirit so we don't burn out.

You see, service, like devotion, has to come from the heart. It has to be pure, not tainted. In the case of the story at the top of this chapter, Caroline resented her position initially, until the love for her mother, and her desire to serve, awakened as a result of her revelation. Service cannot be forced. It has to flow naturally. The heart must awaken to this desire to serve purely and authentically.

Service and Humility

When we reside in humility, we embrace service wholeheartedly, for service and humility fit together like a hand and glove. If we see ourself as part of this chain of existence, what higher joy or fulfillment would there be than to serve? I have heard about humility from many parents, especially with a newborn child. They say being a parent humbles you. Yes, it does, for you are serving another, in every single human way, from cleaning, bathing, and feeding to providing affection and comfort. It breaks us open in ways that humble us, for we see our own fragility, and our fundamental need for each other. We experience the essence of our existence in a larger, universal context. This is humbling.

Humility isn't about not having pride in the self; it's about avoiding the form of pride that is an illusion of our superiority—ego. Many of us reside in maniat (as discussed in Chapter Five); we see ourselves as big people, with big egos, with big me-ness. This is against the grain of the spiritual soldier. Moses, Jesus, Sai Baba, Gandhi, Imam Ali, Buddha, Mother Teresa, and many other great gurus and masters, all sat, ate, and slept among the common people, even though they were at a higher level in their incarnation from a spiritual stance. They understood that the gateway of enlightenment cannot have ego residing in it. To be humble means to see yourself without the crown jewels: without the belief that you deserve, or are entitled to, more than others.

I know a doctor who never mentions she is a doctor. I asked her once, "Why do you tell people you work in a hospital, rather than say you're a doctor?"

"Well, I do work in a hospital," she said.

"Yes," I said, "but you are a doctor. Why not say that?"

"Because that's not important," she replied. "I am simply there to serve, just as the nurses and others are there to serve."

I was so affected by her demeanor and integrity as a soul. She knew if she stated she was a doctor, it might create a divide, since society often perceives professions from a point of status. Without even knowing it, she helped me to better understand humility.

When we release ego, honor others, and live in the kindness and vulnerability of our heart, then humility comes very easily to us. And in this pillar of service, we find the deeper truths in the wisdom traditions, we understand and respect all life, and we see our place in the vastness of the Universe: a single beam of light, amidst an infinite chain of illumination.

The Joy of Service

As we run around collecting our external accomplishments, we may forget to reside in a deeper resonance of humility. Then, as life's events unfold and things happen to us, we find ourselves in uncomfortable situations that call us to "step up" and open some space in our lives. At first this can be a bit of a struggle, for we are so used to our own schedules and timetables. But when we are faced with these situations, we know deep within our hearts that we have to show up and be a *lending hand*.

I remember a friend of mine was always so busy with her life, children, and everyday to-do lists. Suddenly, her brother faced a horrific accident. She had no time to think: she rushed to her brother's side and was with him in each leg of his healing journey. It was very challenging for her at first. She had to not only change her entire life schedule, but also face difficult emotions related to her brother's accident and all of the aftermath that one goes through. She was exhausted, as each day felt like a mountain to climb. But, in her heart she knew she wanted and needed to do this, for him—and also for herself.

Service is like this. It is fulfilling for both the giver and the receiver. Whether we are doing charity work or are called to help someone, a part of us needs to do this for our own sense of inner peace, and also for our personal growth. Many times, we get humbled in the process, for we see life at its most vulnerable, whether taking care of a dying friend or a sick animal, or volunteering with an organization. We are faced with someone in need. We see their fragility, and thus become awakened to the fragility of life itself.

As we slowly walk into this sacred space of service, we gradually come into a quiet joy: a joy that has other colors within it, such as humility, awakening, acceptance, gratitude, and love. This joy is about the peace and Divine Love we feel that flows within us, for we get a glimpse of the sacred thread of life that weaves each of us together. This joy is not always about big laughter, but rather, it is about the quiet reverence of service, flowing within us as a babbling brook, giving us a greater sense of peace, love, and awakening.

The joy of service is beyond fulfilling, for we know we have walked into God's Lap; we know we have served one of God's children and tried to make their life better. No other feeling but service will bring such a sense of purpose, and that is why it is integral to our journey and growth.

As we continue to open our hearts to higher connectivity and love, the practice of service naturally finds its place in our being and will thus flow effortlessly. And as one act of service follows with the next, we develop a new way of being that cements joy and humility in our lives in the sweetest and most profound of ways.

Exercises for Service

- Each day, focus on something that is not about you. It can be watering your garden, or taking a neighbor's dog on a walk, or even as simple as calling a relative who is alone or older. Try doing this for fifteen to thirty minutes each day, and slowly allow more space for it.

- For a week or longer, do not focus on your physical appearance. If you normally wear makeup, forego it, and if you typically try to dress stylishly, opt for comfortable clothes that you usually would not wear in public. As we step away from the focus on vanity, we will feel more comfortable with who we are. This is humbling.

- Write down what causes you are passionate about. See in what capacity you would like to help, then make a plan to be active in it, through volunteering, donating money or resources, etc.

- As you walk in your neighborhood, whenever you see an animal or a person in need, stop. Pay attention to them. Do not look away. Communicate with them. See if you can help them. Do this with love.

In service, we find a fulfillment and joy beyond what we could've imagined. In caring for each other, we are creating a kinder and more humane world. Now, this is a vision to hold on to ...

My beloved sisters and brothers,
I will serve you.
I will serve you, oceans vast and jungles green.
I will serve all who inhabit this sacred Earth.
I will serve with all I am.

I see our oneness,
the thread that weaves us all
in this tapestry of life.
We are mirrors of each other,
as we all carry joy and tears.
I will always be a servant of Love,
in each pulse and in each day.
I will serve with humility
and never will I stray.
This is my highest honor
and my most profound joy.

I sit and bow to this most sacred of paths.

For the first time, Abu was completely quiet. He was in awe of the mules, how they had served people. He felt a deep gratitude fill his being. They were selfless. They expected nothing in return: no accolades or mention. *This was deep*, he thought. *The purpose of our existence is woven with service.* This made him reflect on his life differently and see the makings of the world in an entirely new light. *Our life*, he thought, *is not just about us, but also everyone else. We are all part of one tapestry.*

Chapter Eight

Wisdom

Abu was now having a better understanding of the journey. As each day passed on this path of adventure and self-discovery, he was seeing the dots connecting. His pace had slowed down. He was no longer in a rush like he had been at the beginning. He would stop from time to time, on the way to the next pillar. He would look at the terrain, listen to the rivers, and try to understand the messages of the winds. He had been connecting to the moon and her cycles, and the stars had become his guides, his companions. He would talk to the trees. He had found a deep connection with all that was around and within him. He felt so changed in the last several months. He was seeing everything with new eyes. It seemed that life before the pillars was so far from him now. In each pillar he had unveiled a treasure and found pearls of wisdom. The makings of the Universe, and his own life, were now being reshaped in his soul.

Abu traveled for days. It was him and the quiet, him and nature. He enjoyed each minute. Time was not of the essence, but rather, just a companion.

On a particular day, he saw many animals. He paid attention to their interplays, their actions. He saw the trees and their sway, and watched the breeze touch their leaves. It seemed everything was interconnected, and in as perfect synchrony as a symphony.

The landscape kept on changing. He was in a dense forest now. He could hear the sounds of the animals. He laid underneath a weathered old tree and closed his eyes. He was tired.

"Hoo Hoo." A sound woke him up.

"Hoo Hoo," it repeated.

Abu opened his eyes and got to his feet. The sound kept repeating. He walked past several clusters of trees, following the sound. And then, he saw her: a majestic owl, perched high on the branch of a towering tree. He stepped closer to the tree and raised his head to the owl.

"Hoo Hoo," Abu playfully replied.

The owl hooted again.

"I'm sorry, is this your home?"

The owl was quiet.

"I mean, it's really high up," Abu said, smiling.

The owl remained quiet.

"I guess you don't like to talk much," he said.

Abu turned and walked back to his bags. He took a few steps and stopped, then turned back. He knew!

"You are a pillar, I know you are! And I am sure I know which," he said.

He laughed joyously. *He knew!*

"You are wisdom!" he shouted out loud, excitedly spinning around in a twirl.

The owl looked at him and hooted.

Finally, he had guessed it right! The teachings had sharpened his senses. He smiled, eager to listen to the owl recite the teachings and stories of *The 11 Pillars*.

THE TEACHINGS

"Wisdom is not a product of schooling, but
of the lifelong attempt to acquire it."
Albert Einstein

A dear friend of mine used to put a lot of emphasis on her physical appearance when she was younger. She judged most everyone solely by how they looked. "Pretty" or "ugly" were her typical one-word descriptions of a person, no matter how many compelling personal attributes they may have had. For her, it was always about their looks.

As the years went by, life unfolded with its unpredictable events and it became more difficult for her health-wise, financially, and emotionally. Her marriage dissolved, the kids grew up, and she was left by herself, without the "security" of her youthful looks. Her body was showing signs of aging, and, to her horror, her skin was wrinkling faster than most of her peers. The vanity she had held on to for decades was now wobbly at best, and youth was fleeting, along with her self-image. This made her vulnerable and, in time, more humble, which led to her exploring the facade of overemphasizing one's physical appearance.

She was now searching for meaning and peace, and, for the first time in her life, started looking more in depth into her inner world. She took daily walks and sat in devotion and prayer many nights. And as she spent more time alone, she found new insights into her usual ways of thinking. Eventually, this led her to recognize and appreciate all of the special attributes within herself and others. And with each passing season, she became more awakened and no longer emphasized vanity.

This made her more peaceful and wise, and she even started to *look* more vibrant, for she had discovered a deeper essence to life—one that was not reliant on the physical. She had understood that the ego, or attachment to physical attributes, is not only shallow but transient, and she finally understood that life is so much richer when the focus is, instead, on the deeper essence of the soul. Such is the gift of wisdom.

The Pillar of the Wise

Wisdom is the grandfather of the pillars, as each hard-earned wrinkle speaks of a thousand tales that have been imprinted on the soul's journey. This pillar is integral to our spiritual evolution because, without it, we are as a ship lost at sea. We may be sailing, but we are not directed clearly.

To gain wisdom and truly understand things on a spiritual level, we have to invest in living itself. We cannot experience life from sitting on the couch and alienating ourselves. At the same time, wisdom is not something that accrues just by virtue of extensive life experience. I have met many people in their later years of life who have still not acquired wisdom. We need the awareness and maturity to see life's lessons and teachings, embrace them, and then integrate this newfound knowledge and insight into our daily lives.

This is why the wisdom pillar is not generally cemented in the first half of life. For our first few decades, the spirit is thrust into the exploration of our experiences, trying to grasp things breathlessly. The days and nights are filled with running, trying to catch the wind. Just like fruit that is not yet ripe, we require time in the many seasons of life before the sweet nectar of wisdom will flow. We need to experience the nuance and textures within the painted leaves of autumn, the purity of the winter snow, the dances of the springtime flowers, and the magic of the summer moonlit skies. Only then will the nectar of wisdom tantalize the spirit, quiet the soul, and enrich us with a knowledge based on learning, awakening, growing, and self-realization. Only then will this new paradigm of thought and understanding influence our years and decades ahead, reshaping us slowly and surely, until we ultimately become wiser, more seasoned, more awakened.

Opening Up to Wisdom

Wisdom requires that our soul be open to receive insight, information, and knowledge, and to understand it at a core level. This is largely about seeing and embracing the "higher teachings" of the Universe ... those higher frequencies that are not so apparent to the naked eye but, as a twinkling star, are faint at first, then steadily grow in brightness. Likewise, wisdom approaches us slowly, for it knows the soul cannot be rushed. We need to honor these higher-frequency teachings, these cosmic messages. Once we do, our soul guards them as a treasure, and they become the foundation on which we stand.

To fully access these teachings and insights, we must embrace certain attributes—such as allowance, acceptance, patience, and humility—while simultaneously releasing the ego. The ego cannot thrive in the midst of these attributes, for it is centered around self-righteousness, fear, the false notion of self-preservation, and an unbending attitude toward seeing things in a different way. Wisdom clashes with these negative ideals and, in this duel, the only hero is wisdom: for ego has no substance or depth, yet wisdom is thousands of years old—deeper than the earth itself, and higher than the sky.

Knowledge vs. Wisdom: Is There a Difference?

By definition, knowledge is the accruing of information and the practical understanding of a subject, while wisdom is the quality of having knowledge and insight of a subject, combined with good judgment, and understanding it on a soul level. Is wisdom possible without knowledge? No, for experience by itself does not always guarantee that we will acquire knowledge. Many experience something time and time again, and yet they do not find the knowledge and insight into that subject to create wisdom. Knowledge by itself also cannot attain wisdom. For we can read something, acquire information, and understand it, but that does not solely make us wise. It is the combination of life experience and awareness that helps us to acquire wisdom.

When we go through life, we experience many emotions, events, etc. Each of these can offer many lessons. If we awaken to their deeper meaning, we gain the insight to see the hidden gem inside of each of these experiences, which then supports us in finding the "crown jewel," which is wisdom. Let me give you an example of this.

When I was younger, I took a liking to opera for a period of time. I took lessons and had a few wonderful teachers. But at that point, even though I recognized the value of the teachings and practiced them diligently, I had not awakened to understanding the voice as a powerful instrument or seeing the deeper insight into this art form.

Years later, I met the legendary Persian folk singer, Pari Zangeneh, and was once again learning about singing and vocal expression. In just one session, she explained that it was not only important to sing correctly, but also to understand the significance of the song: its history, expression, and culture. She said each song was a story, and I had to understand the story. She insisted that this was the key element that separated a good singer or artist from a great one. Her words awakened something within me, something I felt I had missed. This awakening led me to the intricacies of the craft, the songs, and the stories and culture that lay behind each one. In this realization, I not only gained further knowledge, but gained a deeper wisdom about this specific level of artistry.

Now, would I have been able to understand what Ms. Zangeneh was speaking about if I had not been a student of music for many years, and had not experienced all the various songs, performances, and teachers? Probably not. For you see, I had to become ripe through my path to awakening, experience, and knowledge. When we gain knowledge, that "knowingness" slowly trickles down into our soul muscles. As our mind awakens to knowledge, our heart awakens to insight, and together they walk into the gateway of wisdom. So, the gaining of knowledge and that deeper understanding and insight is critical to this pillar.

The Truth/Knowledge/Wisdom Connection

Truth is the resonance of a deeper understanding that is critical in obtaining wisdom. It is a springboard into awakening, which is connected to even greater levels of learning and growth. Truth is often most apparent when we're not trying to hide its brilliance, for truth, even when harsh, remains pure in its message. This purity awakens us to deeper insight into our ways, and that of the world around us.

And yet, many people do not want to see the truth of things in their lives, for the truth would make them face aspects that they may feel they are not ready to deal with. But you see, truth always liberates us, for we can break free of the limitations of our perceptions, and in this new insight, obtain the wisdom that our soul yearns for: to be able to enjoy and experience this life in a more liberating and loving way.

A dear student of mine had been in an abusive relationship with a man who was an addict, but did not want to confront and heal his illness. For years, she went through a roller coaster of breakups and make-ups. She was scared to be alone, but also deeply upset that she had spent a good portion of her "fertile" years with this man and still had not had a child. Finally, at the age of fifty-one, when fertility was no longer a valid excuse for her to stay with this man, she broke up with him. I had seen her go through this for years, so when she told me she had ended the relationship I was not truly convinced. But when I saw her a year later, her breakup had stuck. I asked her what had made this time different.

"I wised up!" she said. "I finally got it, like a light bulb went on in me! I saw it for what it was. Why was I blind all those years to the truth of him, and myself? Why could I not see it? No matter how many people told me, I did not want to see it. But suddenly, I did. And once I did, I knew I could never choose it again."

I saw it on her face. She had "gotten it" and, in her own words, she had wised up. The deeper *truth* of the situation finally caught up with her *knowledge* that this relationship had not been supporting her growth and happiness. Some mistake their fear for the truth, so they make themselves believe something that may not be rooted in reality. However, truth is always known to us deep down, underneath the layers of ego and fear: its brilliance can always be seen.

Truth and knowledge are sub-pillars to wisdom. Knowledge always carries truth within it, and truth always creates knowledge. When we see the truth or live our truth, we are finding and understanding knowledge, which then leads us to acquiring wisdom.

The Wisdom Journey

In my personal journey of working with individuals for close to forty years, I have heard many stories, worked with every type of person, from every walk of life, and have been a witness to the vast array of human emotions and thought. Now, in midlife, I can see how my years as an intuit, healer, and teacher have brought me much wisdom, for I learned through every session: I listened, heard the stories, and saw the lessons that were being taught. My heart awakened to these teachings the Universe was generously gifting me.

And so it can be for all of us. As long as we are living and breathing, we can learn from those around us in our everyday experiences; we can observe nature, watch the cycles of the moon, and gain insight into the mechanisms of the Universe; and we can read books and gain knowledge from those who have traveled this road before us. It is all there to assist us in our journey to wisdom, so long as we remain open to the process.

Exercises for Wisdom

As expressed earlier, wisdom cannot be rushed, but there are many different channels we can open to learn and find insight:

- Ask those who are older to tell you their stories of travel and life lessons.

- Read biographies and history books. Study lives of great masters and gurus. Take notes of the key things you have learned.

- Observe the cycle of the moon, sun, and the seasons. Walk outside, be mindful of your surroundings, see the wisdom of the ways of nature. Pay attention to the wind, the trees, the flowers, etc. See their interconnectedness.

- In your meditations, connect to the dreams, teachings, or awakenings you have received.

- In your quiet times, literally envision that you are opening your arms to an expansion of thought, and new perceptions.

- When a cycle keeps repeating, see if your ego is blinding you from seeing the deeper truth. Imagine if you were witnessing a friend going through this cycle. It will help you see more objectively.

- Travel if you can, even if it is close by. Go somewhere you have not been before. Walk into the local stores and places, observe the people and speak to them. Keep a journal on this.

- Be truthful to yourself when you feel disappointed or heartbroken. Rather than think, *Why me?*, see the lesson ... the deeper message. This may awaken you to something you did not see or know.

With these practices, we feel our feet connecting deeper to the wisdom of the sages. In walking through this journey of life, as we remain open to learning, wisdom awakens us. Such is the gift of living and aging with an open heart and mind.

O Great Universe …
You teach me through each breath.

Each tear, each wrinkle, each experience
makes me richer.
Each story, each encounter
is etched in my soul,
awakening me to a higher wisdom.
Through these lessons and teachings,
I walk into new insights and awakenings …
forever-treasures for my soul.
I embrace the pearls of wisdom
You gift me so graciously each day.

And as the hand of time whispers to me,
I find deeper insight and knowledge of Your Ways.

The owl had spoken slowly, yet deliberately, as each word and story held profound weight. *That is what wisdom is*, thought Abu. *The soft whisper, that carries with it only truth.*

Chapter Nine

Gratitude

Abu spent the next several nights in the forest. He watched the owl's stillness and being. He was learning about patience and allowance, and observing life in each moment. He felt he had grown in years. He had loved each pillar and their teachings. Each day and night, no matter how hard the journey had been on him, like a soldier, he had stayed committed and not wavered. Now, he knew he was getting closer to the end of the pillars. He wanted to cherish each moment. He understood this would be the most treasured experience of his young years. And he knew this would help him build a solid foundation for the rest of his life.

The day awakened him with a light rain. Everything smelled new. Spring was budding in the air. Abu felt joyful and refreshed as he began his journey to the next pillar. It was the first time that he saw more wildlife: rabbits and squirrels, frogs and peacocks. Soon, the terrain became even more lush. There were many flowers, bushes, and small trees. Everything was buzzing with life. He sat in the heart of this green oasis and soon after drifted into sleep.

He had a dream. It seemed real. In it, he was right where he was sleeping, and he asked the flowers where the pillar was. They said it was there, a few steps from where he was lying.

Abu got up, and his dream and reality seemed to merge. He looked a bit to the distance. And there, he saw it: a rich patch of soil, budding with a garden full of colorful flowers and plants.

He walked towards it and smiled at the sight of this magnificent bounty and beauty. *This time*, he thought, *I have no idea what this pillar stands for*. And then, he shouted out loud: "I have no idea what you stand for!"

Just then, he heard a voice, deeper than anything he had ever heard, as a rumble, from the depths of the earth.

"You are on the sacred grounds of gratitude," it proclaimed.

Instantly, without thinking, Abu fell to his knees. He felt a holy reverence. Tears of joy and thankfulness brimmed in his eyes. With his head down kissing the ground, once again, he heard the earth rumble.

"You have journeyed long to come here; now ... listen."

Abu laid down on the ground, as he wanted to drink in each word. And thus, the earth began the teachings from *The 11 Pillars*.

THE TEACHINGS

"Gratitude can transform common days into thanksgivings."
Thich Nhat Hanh

In big Western cities, the need to constantly strive for more distances us from the bigger picture of our life and its deeper purpose. I had always seen many of my students and clients grapple many daily life questions, such as why they continued to struggle financially, why they couldn't find their life partner, or why they had yet to connect to their life purpose.

In 2020, our world was rocked by COVID-19. As the year progressed, the pandemic forced us to stay home. We all went inward and began to see our world in a new light. Many started shifting their perceptions of life and its blessings. Before this global pandemic, many had not allowed themselves to sit in this space of reflection and take stock of their lives, as they were busy running around each day. As the number of illnesses and deaths grew, and we all were further distanced from our family and friends, something quite valuable filtrated into our consciousness. We became grateful for *be-ing*, and for being alive. We became aware of the gift of breath, the body, and simple daily activities. We connected more to nature, art, books, music, and inner work. This slowly birthed gratitude in our hearts. We had forgotten how to connect with the Universe, with Source, and even with each other. But now, the reality that life could not be taken for granted became clearer than ever before.

For many, gratitude was the biggest learning point of this time. It transformed us, because it made us realize and understand that our time is the gift. It is to be treasured. Through this awareness, many made decisions to change their life, to create movement, and to release the things that no longer served them: to essentially live a life that was more about being grateful for what they have and less about striving for yet another elusive goal.

The Oxford English dictionary defines gratitude as: "The quality of being thankful; readiness to show appreciation for, and to return kindness." Gratitude is a definitive point we arrive at during our spiritual journey. It takes time to walk into this most profound awareness. As a pillar, gratitude is as the sweet drip of honey on the bread. It is about the love and connection that an open heart both receives and expresses, holding no pain and no regret. It can cause each moment of life's twists and turns to hold a different space and quality: a peaceful, harmonious resonance of deep joy and reverence.

Gratitude is expressed when the spiritual warrior has truly connected to his own breath and, by extension, the essence of the Universe. Without gratitude, we can still do our practice, our meditations, and our prayers. However, these practices will be missing a key factor: a deep thankfulness where we see each moment as a blessing. In this way, gratitude brings us to a higher consciousness, as we become more aware of our actions, thoughts, and way of life, which supports us in stepping into surrender and enlightenment.

The Challenge

Every Thanksgiving, people gather around the dinner table and give thanks for health and family. They take a moment to see through the eyes of love and kindness. The next day, however, they rush into the world of Black Friday and get upset when they cannot obtain a dress, tool, or toy that was on sale. The challenge with this is that we get caught up in these superficial games, which are glorified in our society, but that take us further from the heart of gratitude.

As human beings, we see the glass as half-empty, as we take stock of our lives solely by our achievements and to-do markers. In modern-day society, there is the stress of constantly striving for something more, of "getting to some place." The challenge with this is, we are so focused on getting there, that we miss the stops and the scenery along the way. We become obsessed with the destination, with little regard for the journey to get there.

So, the challenge becomes very apparent to the spiritual seeker. Is obtaining the goal the only objective? Is reaching the destination solely what will help us arrive at a state of bliss? If so, then why do we not feel immense joy when we achieve something? Why does it often feel flat once we get it? Is it not the everyday simplicity and magic of just being alive that can actually be the nirvana we so desperately seek? Is the joy not in the journey itself, the everyday moments of being?

I recall a student of many years past that so wanted to get married and have a child. She became obsessed with this and even had an age in mind that she had to get married by. She found a partner and got married, although there were many red flags and challenges. They were not happy, but thought a child would bring them closer together. Instead, she went on to struggle with both her marriage and motherhood, and was even more unhappy than before. After a few years, she left her husband and child. Unfortunately, this cycle of being driven by a goal was the only way she knew. She never stopped to smell the roses, to take a moment to see the hills and valleys before her. Like a runner on a marathon ticking through mile after mile, she had goal after goal, without a pause in between.

She achieved them all, only to find herself feeling empty at the age of forty. It wasn't until the immense pain she experienced from the loss of a parent that she was awakened to the inner journey of healing, mindfulness and, ultimately, gratitude.

The Gift

In truth, gratitude is about recognizing all that we have is a blessing, a gift. It is not about what we might think we are *deserving* of. It is about truly seeing the gift of life and the endless bounties we have been given. Once we understand this, we understand gratitude. Everything we have, *or do not have*, is a blessing. We need to trust that the Universe gives us what we need for our life and our betterment—at all times. And through this, we will see each facet of our life as a gift, even in the absence or void of something we desire. The gift is in all of it.

The brilliant twelfth-century Persian poet and philosopher Saadi speaks of this:

"Every inhalation of the breath prolongs life and every exhalation of it gladdens our nature; therefore, every breath confers two benefits, and for every benefit gratitude is due."

In the Middle East, when someone asks us how we are, the response is usually, "Thank God," implying there is nothing to complain about. The word "shokr," which means "thanks," is used many times in the day as a response to a question. It reinstates this core belief that at the heart of it all, we are thankful and grateful. In this way, gratitude is a state of being, a mindset, and a perception that slowly, in time, becomes integrated into our daily life.

A Mind Full of Gratitude

Buddhists teach mindfulness in their beginning meditation workshops, for they believe that it is key to living a life of inner contentment. Mindfulness connects us more deeply to the concept of humanity, and embracing each moment more fully. As we understand the gift of each moment, each breath, we become more aware of the choices we make, what we are surrounded by, what we eat, how we live, how we talk, etc. We learn to "respect" the moment, and in this respect, we become mindful, honoring the blessings and gifts, and understanding more deeply how we can choose with more wisdom. Once we understand this, the "joy of the moment" will be intertwined with our breath: a blessing beyond compare.

As we become more mindful at this level, the gratitude in us further accelerates. When we recognize and acknowledge other things or beings, we are taking the focus off of the "me." We're focusing on the unity of the "us" or the "all" that is. Here we understand that, although our individual life is so precious, we are part of the whole, and we step away from any narcissism or self-centeredness (maniat). We understand the "we" that lives in the "I."

The Blessing of the Moment

As we recognize each moment as precious, we experience it more fully. And gradually, as we practice this more and more, it becomes part of our outlook and being.

A cousin of mine was a yoga teacher and each time I visited her, I noticed the long-standing stillness that she practiced before eating. I particularly remember a night where she had a very simple spread of fruit, nuts, bread, and cheese for her students. As we sat to eat, she stated that we should be silent and, through each bite, acknowledge the blessing of eating, of life, and of each other. There were about ten of us, and we each took a piece of bread and then passed the plate on. We closed our eyes, silently gave thanks, and then quietly ate each piece of food, aware of its connection to the earth, its textures and flavors, and the breath of our life and each other.

This birthed a deep stillness and awareness in me. First, I realized how soon my hunger subsided. I did not really need to eat too much, but just needed to take more time with each bite. The warm tea brought my soul into a tranquil state and I understood how each food invites a different sensation within us. In such acknowledgment, I noticed each woman at the dinner table with a sharper vision: their physique and the contour of their mouths as they ate; the sadness or joy they carried as they passed along the food. Without knowing them, I *felt* their stories. And I heard the whispering songs of their hearts.

This new awareness brought with it a beautiful mindfulness. I was recognizing each moment of time with more clarity and experiencing a deeper space of thankfulness. My senses became more heightened, and I became more grateful when I ate, visited a loved one, or even when I took a walk. I hugged more trees, touched more flower petals, and became more mindful of the energy my words carried. I could clearly see the tainted colors, the pain, and the joy, and felt gratitude for all of it, for they were all part of the experience of life itself. And you know what was just as amazing? This never left me: it became ingrained in my soul.

An Ode to Joy!

You may ask yourself, how can joy be part of this key pillar? After all, is joy important to the spiritual evolution we each go through in our life? Is it not perceived as a luxury for the human heart?

No, for you see, gratitude contains joy, a joy that is not always loud like the brass section of a band. Instead, it is as the sound of a piccolo or harp—lovely, as a breeze enveloping us. This joy I am speaking of is a resonance, a vibration: it is a feeling one experiences in the simplest of moments. There is a huge difference when joy is attached to an external element, such as passing an exam with flying colors, or getting a job you have wanted. This joy springs from within and is about the connectivity factor—to Source, to nature, to ourselves, and to one another.

Gratitude births joy and vice versa. This joy is a deep understanding, an awakening of the heart to the light of being. As we connect more to that inner child, we connect more to joy. Once connected, even when sad, that joy is there. How is that possible, you may ask? I will explain.

After the passing of a father figure in my life, I felt sad and I missed him. But each day I felt a gratitude … a joy of having been blessed with his presence and love. Although sad at the loss, I was so grateful for the years with him, my heart held a quiet joy. The joy was serene yet constant, and would put a smile in my heart, although my eyes held tears.

As we go through the trials and triumphs of life, we come to understand the essence of being is not in suffering—although that is also part of our journey—but in ultimately basking in the joy of just being. The fact that life contains lessons and struggles is a given. Some of us have more to overcome than others: this is the way it is. Based on your belief system, it can be karmic, or just a reality of your current journey. Either way, life in its essence is about the glory and the fall. The tears and laughter. It is all connected. Our challenge as human beings is to open our hearts to this connection and see with the eyes of our souls. Once we do, then joy and gratitude will be integrated into our every moment and in our every breath.

Exercises for Gratitude

- Each morning when you wake up, take a look outside the window. See the sky, the trees, or whatever is there. Greet the day by welcoming it into your life and take a few moments to give thanks. Inhale and exhale the blessing of being.

- During the day, become aware of the gift of breath, of life, and of your various experiences. Take a moment or two to connect to all that is and all that you have, remembering that all you have *or do not have* is a blessing.

- When you sit to eat, take a moment to give thanks for the food. As you eat your food, be mindful of where it came from. Give thanks to the earth for it. Take each bite slowly, appreciating the textures and flavors. Notice how each bite resonates within you.

- When you step outside, pay attention to the people on the street. If someone is in need of food or help, assist them. This is a shared blessing for you both.

- When you are out in nature (or in a garden or park), close your eyes, put your hand on your heart, feel the beat, let the air fill up your lungs, see the child within you, connect to it, and feel the joy of being present, of being alive.

- Do something each day, for yourself or someone else, that makes you smile or gives you joy. If you can find more than one thing, then embrace and allow it.

- Don't throw your food, clothes, or other belongings away. Give these things freely to others, and feel the joy of giving.

- Each night when you lay in bed, take a breath in, and as you exhale, give thanks for the gift of that day—no matter if it was easy or hard—as you greet the hours of sleep and rest ahead.

Gratitude is the ultimate gift we can give ourselves. It is in this reverence that we can see the light and beauty in everyone and everything, and in our own being. As the heart resides in gratitude, the regrets, anger, and all ill feelings subside, and what is left is only joy. In this realization, each experience of life becomes so much richer, and the most simple of acts become poignant moments of joy and remembrance. The moment not repeating, is as the breath, a gift we cannot take for granted.

ʃ

Beloved,
My heart resides in the deepest of gratitude
and is filled with immense joy,
embracing the gifts
You bestow upon me each day.
How blessed am I to see
and bask in this beauty and love!
My heart sings in delight!
Each moment, each breath, each pulse
fills me with eternal joy and gratitude.
I bow to You,
to Your earth and skies,
humbled and in awe of all I behold.

ʃ

Abu heard the generous earth. He felt the joy of gratitude as a tree growing within him, full of richness. He looked around, noticing every particle of nature. He felt his being was smiling, bowing to the skies and waters, creatures and Earth. A joyous light filled him. At last ... he felt at home, connected to all.

Chapter Ten

Surrender

Abu basked for days in this luscious landscape. He watered the flowers, talked to the plants, and hugged the trees. He lay on the earth and listened to her pulse. He felt a deep connection to each and every thing around him.

Abu was not in a rush. He was in a joyous mindfulness, embracing each moment of the path. He understood this was a *privilege*, not a search. It was an *honor*, not a chore. It was a sacred pilgrimage for his soul. He felt a deep sense of gratitude, knowing this experience was the most profound blessing he could receive.

Finally, one spring day as the sun and rains were at play, Abu continued his journey. *I will miss this place*, he thought. "I will carry it each day within me," he whispered, smiling. It was now part of his inner landscape.

After many months, once again, there was a hazy mist in the air, making the unknown terrain difficult to navigate. At times, Abu would sit, waiting for the fog to clear. It felt like he was going in circles, getting nowhere. One particular night, he felt completely lost. He closed his eyes, took a breath in, and then exhaled. He was resetting himself, connecting to the light center within him. He envisioned the stars wrapping around him, heard the chanting of the hayfields and the music of the waterfalls, and remembered the ants and their determination. He felt a reconnection to all of these teachings and pillars.

Although the road and the mist were not clearing, he resumed. A few days later, he started to feel the frustration again. He was sure at this stage it would have gotten easier to find the pillars. The thought kept entering his head: *Is there no end? Is there always more to grasp, learn, evolve into?*

He suddenly paused. A light bulb turned on in him. *Yes*, he thought. *That is it! We are here to constantly grow and evolve ... until we stop breathing.* He understood it now.

Finally, on day eight, he gave into the splendor of just not knowing where he was going. This freed him to fully trust the journey. He had faith. He had belief. And he had obtained this wisdom after all these months, understanding that things are not always as they appear.

Smiling, feeling grateful for being lost in the rivers and swamps, he felt that joy once again of just being present, in the moment.

Abu opened his arms and shouted out, "I love you, world! I give in to the splendor of being, oh great Universe! I surrender to you! I surrender to Your glory!" And just as he said those words, he heard a flock of birds soaring above his head.

They were circling around him. He was astounded. His jaw dropped open. And as they flew, he saw the most amazing sight. There was a sanctuary of sorts made of branches and leaves, and on each branch, there were more birds. It was as a big house of birds! *Oh wow! This must be a pillar!* Abu thought.

He ran to it, enthusiastically. He looked at the birds, some flying, some sitting on the tiny branches. He moved closer.

"Salam, salam!" he said, out of breath. He was so thrilled to be there with them.

"Salam," they sang back to him, melodically.

"May I ask what pillar this is?" he said, smiling at the beautiful, musical greeting.

He was truly curious, for he knew by now that each journey had prepared him for the next pillar.

"Surrender," they chirped back at him.

Abu kneeled in reverence. He felt an indescribable grace. He opened his arms and looked to the skies. The birds came and sat on his arms and head. Smiling from ear to ear, with his eyes closed and his heart open, Abu listened as they melodically read from *The 11 Pillars*.

THE TEACHINGS

"For we have not come here to take prisoners or to confine our wondrous spirits, but to experience ever and ever more deeply our divine courage, freedom, and Light!"
Hafez

A dear friend of mine had been in the process of adoption from her native country for years. The roadblocks were many, and each one would lead her to a dead end. She would then pursue another route of adoption, which would also become a dead end after a couple of years. She was devastated, for each turn of the past decade in following her dream had resulted in a heartbreak. Now in her midlife, she was losing all hope.

For a while, she let it be. She did not know how to live without this dream, and yet, she did not have much push left in her. Depleted financially and emotionally, she and her husband let it go. As a person of strong faith, she turned to God, but she could not understand her fate. Although she did not close her application file, she surrendered it and continued her life.

A while later—after she had released it to the Universe and accepted her fate of not having a child—she got a call out of the blue that changed everything: she could become the foster mother of not one, but *two* baby sisters from a completely different place than her home country. She fully embraced this. The Universe had not forgotten her. There was a plan for her after all: a different one, at a different time than she had imagined, but a plan, nonetheless.

In this process of our spiritual evolution, we now walk into a pillar that is a testament to all we have learned, practiced, and awakened to—surrender. In life, we often have an inner battle: a struggle that may develop between the heart, mind, ego, and/or external beliefs. Surrender is the optimal place where human beings can arrive, for it opens us to total acceptance, allowance, and trust.

The reason surrender is so important in the more evolved spiritual practices, is because it is the final leap in understanding the connectivity between ourself and the Universe. In Arabic, the word "taslim" is used to express surrender, which is all about *stepping away* from the control and agenda of the ego, and having complete trust of the Universe. As we close our eyes and open our arms, we feel the winds in our chest, and trust that whatever might come to pass, we will always be lifted to find flight in the way intended for our journey.

Imagine a heavy storm where there is no electricity, so we light a candle and sit in its glow. We are afraid of the destruction the storm can bring, and we worry about our loved ones who are out in the storm. We desperately want to control the storm and the events it may bring forth. But in truth, we cannot. We need to surrender and allow the storm to find its way to calm, for we cannot control the electricity or where our loved ones are. It is out of our hands and in the hands of the Universe. This is what surrender is. Is it easy? Of course not. But does this deepen the connection to the Divine and to ourself? Yes. Does this free us? Yes. Does this support our faith even more? Yes. Are there any drawbacks to this level of surrender? No, not even one.

Choosing to Trust

The main challenge of this pillar is the trust aspect: the allowing and accepting of the Ways of the Universe, even if we do not like them. This trust has to be cemented slowly, with faith and patience being key elements in leading us to surrender naturally and most gracefully.

When we fall in love, we give in to the splendor of it, we allow it. And so it is to surrender. It is sublime to see ourself as part of the Universe, and to bend to the Ways we are guided to, just as the trees and rivers do.

There is a saying in my native country—"har chi salahe, khast Khodasst"— that means, *Whatever is best for us is God's will.* This is said when we are at a crossroads or questioning something. It is basically saying *God knows best*, or, *In Him we trust.* This level of trust is critical, for without it, we cannot truly surrender.

In acting classes, there is a great exercise where one person stands with another behind them, and then they allow their body to fall backwards, trusting that they will be caught. Surrendering is exactly this: a deep trust, knowing we will be caught.

Giving In to Wisdom

The main misconception about surrendering is how some view it as synonymous with giving up. This cannot be further from the truth. Surrender is not about giving up, but rather, giving in to the wisdom of the Universe. It is about a deep level of trust, understanding, and humility. The biggest obstacle to getting to this beautiful plateau of being and thought is the ego, for the ego has a hard time giving up control, or allowing for the opening of a higher wisdom. The ego also looks down on humility because it cannot allow another viewpoint or perspective, let alone saying, *This is no longer in my control.* In a world of chaos and, at best, unpredictability, the ego tightly holds the reins to control situations and outcomes. Yet, anyone who has lived life past youth knows that control is an illusion of the mind: We can no better control the outcome of things than we can control the rain, the sunshine, or the storms.

Even spiritual practitioners who have devoted much of their lives to enlightenment may still be working on this pillar. In my life, I have met a few souls who, although young in their biological years, have in their depth grasped this pillar, even if the practice of it usually takes years or even decades to master. For surrender has to be deeply understood on a soul level, and this is very much connected to our trust, belief, and understanding of the Universe.

All of this said, surrender does not mean we don't work hard at something. It means we work hard and do our best, but then surrender the results of our efforts—which are often out of our control—and allow these results to flow as It sees fit.

Embracing Detachment

Releasing expectations and creating detachments are a strong part of this pillar. It is when we have attachment to outcome that we usually do not surrender, for we then focus on getting something we currently do not have. The concept of expectation can also, in its depth, hold a sense of entitlement, of being "deserving of something." Many feel they have earned the right to something, that years of their diligence has entitled them to a spot or space. In truth, this concept holds no place in spiritual evolution, for it takes us away from gratitude, contentment, and ultimately, surrender itself. To be hopeful in life and look forward to the outcome we desire, is quite different than expectation.

Simply put, we should not attach ourself to the idea of expecting a reward or a particular outcome when we do something. We may work hard at things, but the idea of feeling we *deserve* something does not align with surrender, spiritually. In understanding the Universe and our place in it, we have to see that life does not necessarily give us what we expect, feel entitled to, or "deserve," and to set ourself up for such an outcome allows us to feed our ego, not our humility.

Ego tells us that more is what is important, and to expect rewards and accolades. But humility is content with what is. And while the humble, hard-working person may be hopeful to receive the rewards and feel they have earned it, they do not attach themself to this expectation, for they feel no need to control an outcome. Instead, they trust the process will unfold organically.

Additionally, detachment from connections to the material world is key to our spiritual evolution. Many create attachments to physical things like their home or their car. Those things are fleeting and impermanent. And yet, detachment is not a bad word. It does not mean we do not have affection or passion for something, but rather, that we understand this physical world is temporary and we cannot attach ourself to its fundamental impermanence.

To take this a step further, we should not attach ourselves to other people, for we understand that, although we are all links of one chain, we are each separate in our journey here. To quote a line from Kahlil Gibran's poem on marriage; "Stand together, yet not too near together: for the pillars of the temple stand apart, and the oak tree and cypress grow not in each other's shadow." Now, you may ask, *Well, I am attached to my mother, is that bad?* No, it is not bad, as long as we understand that loving is not the same as attachment, and that we can love without feeling a sense of dependency on another for our peace of mind and inner happiness.

A dear friend of mine was deeply attached to her parents. She had lived with them all of her life, to fifty years of age, and her daily activities revolved around them. When they were down, she was down; when they were sick, she suffered with them. As they began to grow older and weaker, she had to face the inevitable. This was difficult for her, but she slowly started doing things she loved, finding new friends, and building a life for herself. In time, she became more detached from the feeling that her welfare depended solely on her parents, and even took trips without them, as she began to pursue her desires. She still loved her parents with all of her heart and continued to take the best care of them, but her welfare was no longer dependent on their well-being.

Mastering detachment is a process of time, so it does not usually come to those early in life. But those who spend time in devotion, understand detachment. For when we understand Creation, we see that our purpose in life is to find joy, to awaken, to evolve, and to serve. In realizing this, we detach ourself from expectations, from codependency, and especially from things that are frivolous. In time, this detachment actually connects us to the most important thing: our own spiritual essence, connected to that of the Universe.

Allowing Allowance

Everything begins with allowance. When we give ourself permission to experience inner freedom, we allow ourself to see through the eyes of our heart and wisdom, and we walk into a new threshold: that of surrender, which derives from the allowance to give up control. As humans, allowance is not only about us opening the gates to a new way or perception, but also being open to trusting the process, and hoping for, but not attaching ourself to, a particular outcome. This is not easy for us, for we falsely believe we are losing our power. But in truth, once we allow ourself to be open and trust this journey, we will see the visions will change, we will change, and even the outcomes will change.

In a period of my life when I had retired from one-on-one work, I allowed an openness to see what would find *me*. A story found me and, as I embraced it, I found myself at a threshold of a very new endeavor: to make a short film. This led to many months of collaborative work, and, along the way, I had created expectations that could not be realized. And in the final months, as the process became frustrating and my expectations and vision had changed, the project came to a halt, and I surrendered to the majority vote.

Naturally, I was disappointed at first, but after the disappointment wore off a few days later, I saw the truth of it all: and there, in that, I felt liberated. In allowing the process, I had learned a lot and, although the project never got to the finish line, I had made amazing contacts, met incredible people, and discovered a new art form.

In the days that followed, I had a creative breakthrough and rewrote the project, feeling even further liberated, and knowing it could now take flight without me holding onto its wings. It was then I realized that in allowing a door to open, we have to allow the creation its own unique journey and set it free to become whatever it is intended to become. We must allow it to find its own wings and fly as it wishes, even if it turns out differently than what we had hoped. This is ultimately what every parent learns in raising a child: to trust that the child will find their own wings and fly.

Those who practice surrender know that it holds a peace without measure, for they have trusted this Universe, which is our home, trusted the Ways, which guide us, and trusted our place in this Divine Sphere. This peace obtained does not contain ego, seek to control, or expect a particular outcome. It is as a bird, free in its flight, trusting the winds. This peace is the biggest gift we can give to ourselves.

Key Exercises for Surrender

- Have someone stand behind you. Close your eyes and fall back. This will help you build strength and inner confidence in your trust.

- Take a drive without having a particular destination in mind. Let the road take you on a journey, and embrace this process. Take in the new settings and scenery, and observe how you experience something new and unexpected. Stop and step out of your car, when you can. What may unfold or who you may encounter, will open you up to new visions.

- Allow yourself to do something in your daily schedule that you would not normally do. Sleep late or go to bed early; enjoy a new type of food you normally wouldn't eat; engage in a new activity—such as a type of exercise—that you may have no interest in. Practice this each week, allowing for something different. Pay attention to what you learn from it and how it may have shifted your perception.

- Do something like go to a movie, or take a day trip with a person or group you normally would not socialize with. Step outside of your comfort zone and detach yourself from its outcome. Just be in the moment, experiencing it.

- Catch yourself when you are attaching yourself to an outcome. Breathe out any sense of control or expectation, and embrace openness and joy. Inhale and exhale several times, physically open your arms, and repeat, *I trust*.

- Once a week, wake up without any plan for that day. Sit in the gratitude of the moment. See what may unfold. Allow and embrace it.

The ultimate gift we can give ourselves is to walk slowly into this new plateau of surrender, opening our hearts and wings, and saying, "I trust the flight, I trust the sail, I trust the Ways." In this, we finally become free and connect to life, in the most magical of ways.

૬

Oh wings,
trust the flight!
Live not in fear of what may be,
worry not of the storms and hails.

Trust the sail ...
It will take you to where is intended
for you.

Open your arms ...
See before you the endless vastness.
You are part of this beauty,
You are born to be this ...
Free ...
You are the flight itself.

Abu sat in awe, contemplating surrender ... the freedom of the flight. He watched the birds fly high and felt mesmerized by their lightness of being. They seemed to exude so much grace, joy, and surrender. *How beautiful is it to be this?* thought Abu. *I will become this, maybe not today or tomorrow ... but in time.*

Chapter Eleven

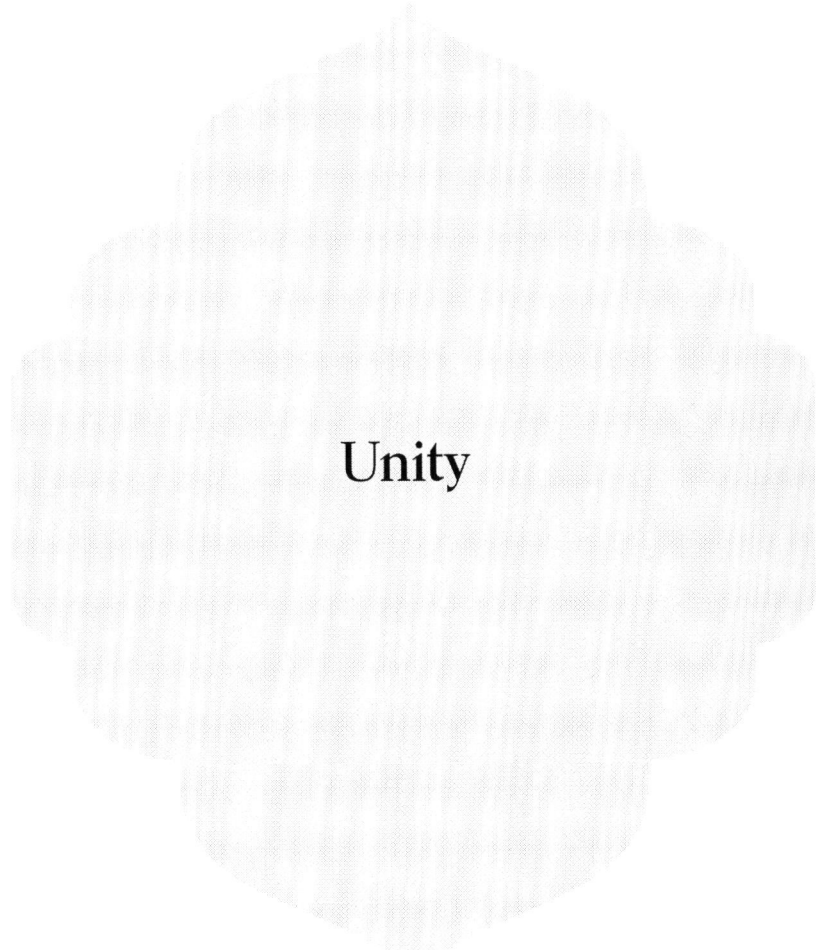

Unity

For weeks, Abu stayed near the rivers and swamps. He was embracing each day and night with such gratitude, trusting his journey would unfold as intended. Gone was the angst, the rush, and the frustration.

One night, as the full moon was filling up in her glory, Abu was in the deepest of sleep, when a vision he had about the pillars from of a year ago found him once again. But this dream held a different message. He saw the journey, each pillar; he saw the owls and stars, the hay and ants, the deer and dogs, the garden and waterfall, and the donkeys and birds. He then saw himself on the dirt road after the last pillar. A middle-aged monk-like man sat at the end of the road. He resembled the old man he had seen at the beginning of his journey. Without looking at Abu, the man said, "Now that you have seen and heard it, go live it. Each day, walk *into* the pillars, until you become them." Then he disappeared into the haze.

Abu jumped up from the earth beneath him. His pulse was beating strong. The night sky was a velvet blue, filled with stars, and the enticing moon glowed in her fullness. The owls were howling, the birds were singing, and all seemed to be orchestrated in the most remarkable masterpiece. *Yes*, he thought, *this is the symphony of life*. Tears of deep joy ran down his face, as he felt a love for All envelope him once again into a blissful sleep.

The time had come, once again, for Abu to continue his journey, this time to the last pillar. The terrain ahead contained everything: land and trees, hills and valleys, rivers and streams. Abu relished each moment, each step. He ate from the shrubs and drank from the springs and bathed in the waterfalls. He slept under the stars, and played with the animals. Joy filled his being, a love indescribable.

The days went by, and soon it became a week, then two. The landscape soon filled with trees standing tall next to each other. He saw a huge herd of elephants, with zebras and buffaloes close by. Abu took rest under a big tall tree. When he woke up, he saw many animals around him, including rabbits, frogs, squirrels, and monkeys. He laughed and said out loud, "Oh, this is so magical! I know you are not a pillar, but I'm so happy to be here with you!"

"We *are* a pillar," said a commanding voice from a tree. Startled, Abu jumped to his feet.

"Who is the pillar?" Abu asked.

"We all are," said the tree.

Abu was speechless for a minute. "What pillar are you all?" he asked.

"We are Unity."

Abu bowed his head to the earth and skies and All Creation.

The animals gathered around him, and soon the tree began to recite from *The 11 Pillars of Self-Realization.*

THE TEACHINGS

"All see themselves in You and they see You in everything."
Attar of Nishapur

The first several months of COVID-19 there was a sense of shock, as anxiety and depression started to set in globally. I would constantly get emails and texts from everyone wanting to know when things would become normal again. I could tell many were struggling, as the fear of the illness and, for many, the aloneness factor, were quite tough to go through.

I decided to do a weekly remote prayer/meditation/visualization video session. For close to two months, we would come together "virtually" every Friday. We were from various regions of the world. We were Moslems, Christians, Agnostics, Jews, and Buddhists. We were Democrats and Republicans. And yet, we were not. In those thirty to forty minutes, we were simply a group of vulnerable souls coming together during a period of heightened stress, looking to experience release, find our footing, and connect to one another. We were united in this intention and, in our togetherness, we all understood that what was most important was to simply be present for the group. And in this unity, we gathered uncommon comfort and strength. It was quite beautiful, transformative, and healing.

Imagine a painting of a beautiful piece of nature: we see the trees, mountains, and hillsides. We see the green grass and pebbles, the rivers, birds, and butterflies. We are part of this painting, too, if we allow our vision to look beyond the canvas. And collectively, we are part of something we call Universe, or God, or Creation. And it is in seeing this Grand Connection, that we understand we are responsible for *all of this*, each other, and ourselves.

The unity pillar cannot usually be cemented early in life, for it requires a certain level of maturity and wisdom, along with deep insight and understanding into the makings of life, and our place in the Universe. When we speak of unity and interconnectedness, we are speaking not only about our connection to our fellow humans, but also our connection to All that is.

Many of us live in modernized societies where the focus is very much on the I: the individual. We create the neutral family and have a select number of friends or groups with whom we interact. We are each "in a bubble" and living our own individual life. Yet, as we come to understand surrender, gain wisdom, and reside in gratitude, we begin more and more to "see" through the eyes of the soul, which has awakened to the Great Unseen: an understanding that, in life, we are all energetically united, interconnected as a chain—to the earth, trees, animals, and rivers—and each of us creates a domino effect to the other. We are all part of the Great Symphony, as each of us adds our own unique color. If we cannot see this interconnection—this Cosmic Unity—then we have not, in a sense, understood the essence of "being." And we remain in a cubical that has essentially separated us from the rest of Existence.

Hundreds of years ago, we may have slept on a paper-thin mattress, or walked barefoot many miles to visit one another. What this did was consistently remind us of our connection to the earth, and each other. However, as we have now created more cars, technology, fancy shoes, and mattresses, and we now eat at dining tables with forks and knifes, and take vacations in luxury spas, we have missed out on experiencing our interconnection to nature and, in a way, to each other.

I remember going back home to Iran many years ago and eating from a spread that was laid out on the floor. I watched my friend's father eat with his hands. He said the food tasted even richer that way. I tried this and so loved the textures, and the connection of my fingers to the food. There was something so pure and authentic about it. It was as if I was eating from the Earth Herself—so much more fulfilling than eating at any five-star restaurant. It was a joy to eat with him at this simple spread, as we shared the blessings of the earth with one another.

I also recall a visit with a student where we sat on an old rug and talked and talked. We did not look at the clock or have our cell phones with us. We had no knowledge of how many hours had gone by. We were just present with one another, not rushing, but rather, embracing this togetherness. In such priceless experiences, we see our interconnectivity and thus, our unity.

And yet, our unity does not mean we are all of the same thought, but it does mean we are all here, breathing and existing. In this way, we are all the same. The Universe is as one huge womb and we are all *in* it, not separate *from* it. When we really understand this, then those things that appear divisive do not actually separate us. The labels and categories do not define the richer and deeper essence of who we truly are in this infinite thread of Existence: billions of uniquely created charms—and we are, each one of us, one of them.

Barriers to Unity

When I was three, I asked my mom, "Did God create all of us?"

"Yes," she replied.

And then I said, "So, that means we are all here to love one another, for we are all created by God."

Once again, the pure soul of a child knows such truths, and it is later—as the ego, fears, and all other barriers set in—that we lose sight of what we knew long ago.

The ego is often the culprit when it comes to stunting our evolution spiritually, emotionally, mentally, and even, at times, physically. For the ego is governed by false perceptions such as pride, narcissism, and control. The ego creates a separation from truth, for it believes that by separating or seeing itself "above" others, it is more special. In wanting to believe we are special, the ego will look down on others or even attempt to drive them away.

Yet, as individual entities, we *are* special. Just as in nature, there is the elm tree, along with the palm, cedar, and maple. They each have their own unique design, no more or no less. Some of us like the cedar, some the maple, but none rank greater in hierarchy in the realm of the Universe. Perhaps they are not equal in how exactly they serve the Universe, or even in their subjective beauty. But they each *are* and because they *exist* they are each a part of the chain, part of the "womb"—the Oneness.

Celebrating Togetherness

We are all here in a sense to support each other in this journey of life, as we learn from one another, teach one another, and love one another. And through these experiences we evolve, we become whole. For example, we teach babies, but we also learn from them; we tend to trees and flowers, but learn from them, as well. Such is the magic of this miraculous existence.

If we can understand that all of us, as a people, feel, think, and are here to grow, then we can begin to see beyond the walls and facade of it all. For beyond our physical shell is the soul: a soul that has come to experience life in this plane. Yes, some of us may be here as an "Einstein" to serve through science, or a "Picasso" to color the collective senses: some as mothers, others as teachers, and so forth. But we are all here to learn and evolve.

This is our common denominator. And once we see this, it is our responsibility not to allow the ego to divide us through its prejudice and fear. It is only when we refuse to see this truth that we constantly create the divisions. This responsibility is not an obligation. It is birthed out of love and caring for each other. It is about celebrating our togetherness as being part of this divine painting: one family ... one thread.

We Are as One

Saadi, Persian philosopher and poet of the medieval period, said:

> "Human beings are members of a whole,
> in creation of one essence and soul.
> If one member is afflicted with pain,
> other members uneasy will remain.
> If you have no sympathy for human pain,
> the name of human you cannot retain."

The true significance of this poem is this: We each have a life force, an individual energy field, but we are also part of a grander, massive energy: equal parts of a grand chain. When one of us breaks, so do the others; when one of us feels pain, so does another. In fact, we can feel each other's pain, even if we do not see one another. When there is a large fire, even when it is not in our city, we can imagine the trees burning. This greatly pains our spirit. When there is an earthquake or devastation in another part of the world, we lose sleep, cry, and feel the pain of those we have never seen.

Have you ever attended a funeral? When a person cries, their tears move you to tears. The same is true of laughter; it is contagious. This is because we understand each other on a core level. Our pain and triumphs are shared, as are our joys and tears. We are all born, walk our life journey, and then travel to another journey when our hearts cease to beat. The journey is the same, just the stops may be different.

Unity, togetherness, and seeing all as one means we do not always have to see eye to eye on things—we are still brothers and sisters in our differences. Likewise, we don't need to attend the same church or synagogue, or even need to be of the same culture or species. We just need to understand that all of us are forever connected. This is why understanding unity is critical to both our survival and evolution.

Key Exercises for Unity

- Go into a forest or hillside. See each component of nature; the animals, trees, flowers, etc. Honor each of them by seeing them as part of this tapestry of life, just as you are.

- When you see a person, see the light within them. See the child within them. After a few days, you will no longer notice their age, ethnicity, or even gender. You will just see them as beams of light.

- Each day do one thing that makes life better for someone. It can be as simple as assisting somebody in the grocery store, or helping out a neighbor. Do it because you want to. This will deepen your connection to unity.

- Eliminate from your vocabulary such phrases as, "It is not my problem," or, "They are a different breed," etc. Start seeing everyone as one tribe.

- Befriend someone who is quite different than you, either much older, younger, or of a different background. Get to know them, and see the common denominators you share.

- In each person, animal, tree, body of water, etc., see their unique light and how it brings illumination into our world.

In unity, we see the godliness and most sacred of energies—the chain of light throughout the Cosmos. As this light is all around and within us, we come to truly grasp this understanding that unity is about how we each connect to the whole, how each of us are that drop in this ocean of being: Each a star in the endless skies, shining bright. And together, we make this beautiful masterpiece called Existence, a light-filled space of Love.

꜄

O Great Unseen ...
Your jungles and waters,
Your deserts and hills,
Your rocks and streams,
Your animals large and small ...
All divinely designed
are made of Love ...
and love itself.
How blessed are we to belong
to one another,
to be of one tribe,
and of one Womb ...
Never alone,
eternally loved,
forever connected ...
Such is the grace
You have bestowed upon us.
We sit in this unity,
in reverence of All that is,
and all we are to one another,
with the deepest of gratitude.
Amen

Abu listened wholeheartedly, not missing a beat. He took it all in: the trees, animals, streams, skies, and each pebble. He realized that this journey had been one magnificent gift. His dream had guided him to this magical treasure of *The 11 Pillars*, a glorious wisdom of the ages. He would carry these teachings within him and strive to *become* each pillar. This would be his quest.

Epilogue

Abu sat at the entrance of the pillars. The night sky, filled with stars, still stirred his heart with such joy and serenity. He felt *the magic* as he recalled the journey, each pillar, each story, each teaching. He had lived his life with them, they had become his constant companions. And through living and loving, joy and pain, struggle and growth, he had become the avid student, utilizing all the exercises and tools, the wisdom of the pillars in his everyday life.

Gradually, he had become a revered teacher, a servant of Love, traveling far and wide, to small pueblos and big cities, modern places and old, sharing the teachings, spreading the stories and messages. What a profound gift it had been!

Three decades later, he had returned to the pillars, his home. He was at the entrance and exit. He remembered the old man, the young lad, and the monk … his compatriots. All were one, that was the beauty of it all.

Abu took a breath in as he leaned on his stick, and looked to the velvet blue sky as the haze was coming in.

> A key turned …
> Abu's eyes twinkled.
> Excited, he sat patiently.
> A soul was about to walk in
> to find awakening.

A star danced above in the night sky.

Resources

A Brief Guide to Meditation

Meditation is a holistic discipline, a technique that brings us into a space of tranquility and peace, and further guides us to a place of higher awareness and consciousness.

Meditation can be done at any time of day, but it's best to do when the stomach is not full.

Your meditation experience may be different each time. The key is to not judge yourself.

Types of Meditation

1. Traditional Meditation: This can be done sitting or lying down. You can close your eyes or have them open. Start with inhaling the breath for a couple of counts and exhaling it. After a couple of times, elongate the breath and the exhalation. Your mind will slowly let go and you will find a more peaceful state of being.
Note: Start with five minutes a day, and build on this.

2. Walking Meditation: Go for a walk, preferably in silence. Each step you take, you will be further away from the "thought process."
Note: Start with ten minutes and increase this.

3. Candle Meditation: Light a candle, and focus on the flame. As you sit in this space, your mind will slowly let go of thought, and ease into meditation. Use your breath to support this.

4. Object Meditation: Focus on a single object. Slowly, your thoughts will drift away. Use your breath to support you.

The Four Stages of Meditation

1. Allowing and intending meditation, sitting in silence, using the breath.

2. Thought process decreases (each time this may be different, do not judge it).

3. "Meditative state" takes place.

4. Connection to Source or higher consciousness occurs. (Please note this final stage may not always happen.)

Note 1: Nature sounds such as waterfalls, or bamboo flute and light music, can help support your meditation. Many also may prefer absolute silence.

Note 2: Whatever occurs in your meditation, whether it is a message, or something is revealed to you, or you connect to a higher wisdom, allow it.

Meditation will support your well-being on all levels. It is the forever treasure. It has no limits. It is for everyone, anywhere, at any time.

Mantra Practice: An Overview

Mantra, or "zikr," is a word or phrasing that is repeated, and in its repetition, it helps us to find the pathways of deeper connections to the Source, and to our self-realization.

Whether the word(s) are chanted or spoken out loud or in silence, they create a resonance. This supports the unveiling process, releasing the debris, aiding in our purification and healing, and thus, helping our confidence, clarity, and inner peace, as our faith is strengthened and our connection to Source is deepened.

Finding Your Mantra

You can choose a mantra from a wisdom tradition.
You can create your own mantra.
You can receive a mantra from a guide, teacher, or guru.

How long does one do a mantra?

This is partially up to you. When a mantra is given to you by a teacher, they will usually ask you to do it for at least forty days, with a specific amount of minutes in each daily practice. The reason for this is that it takes time for the mantra to work through you.

However, if it's a mantra of your own choosing, I would generally recommend that you practice it twice a day, for one- to five-minute intervals.

Please note: It is in the repetition of the word or phrasing that make mantras most effective. Also, mantras can unveil and create various emotions: allow them to unfold. The mantra will take you on an inner journey, and will bring you to a higher consciousness of being in time.

Other Resources

My first book, *Miraculous Silence,* goes into detail about the practices of meditation and mantra. It also has an index with many mantras from various traditions. Further, there is information on sacred space, visualization, and stone healing.

You can find this book online, in both written and audio formats.

My website is continually updated. You can also subscribe to my newsletter there. Go to: www.voiceofmitra.com

Servants of Love

Servants of Love is a training program I created in 2017 for those who wish to deepen their spiritual path and lead a life of service. This program is about embracing the teachings of the pillars and committing to a life of spiritual service.

This process will take time, as it requires utilizing the exercises and tools, doing the meditation and mantra practices, and devoting time to self-realization, purification, and healing. The program has been designed for the dedicated soldier who yearns for this in their soul, and who will embrace this most sacred of journeys: one of devotion, discipline, and service.

The key component to begin with is the *call to this*. Once you feel this, then the allowance, discipline, and patience for it will follow. This process can take up to a year or more, depending on each person. But the commitment to it is a way of life, of daily being.

For those who are called to this, you can periodically access this url for more information: www.voiceofmitra.com/servantsoflove

Acknowledgments

My heartfelt gratitude to:

Bobby Rock—who stood by me in this four-year process, as this book unveiled. For his guidance, impeccable editing skills, brilliant insights, knowledge, and unconditional support.

Mark Swift—for editing this manuscript with grace, precision, and skill.

Morgane Leoni—for her amazing cover design and gorgeous layouts throughout the book.

A most special thank you to:

Rama Morovati, my devoted husband, for his belief, support and love throughout this journey.

Minoo Rahbar, my precious sister, for her support, insight and keen eye.

Chela Reyna, my magical one, for her love, unwavering support, and valuable input.

And to these beautiful souls for their belief and support (in no particular order):

Kristin Hahn, Jackson Galaxy, Kelli Miller, Dr. Catherine Scott, Gurutej Khalsa, Claudina Bonetti, Matti Buccini, Ruth Sharone, Ana Lovelis, Mohtadi Mirak, Omar Noorzay, Gordafarid, Sima Cohen, Kamran Mohanna, Janet Sode, Jasmine Gharavi, Hannah Alocozy, Nathaniel Eros, and Marzieh Mirzaei.

With all my love ...

> To my beloved mother, who taught and inspired me with her love, knowledge, and wisdom, and opened me to a world of poetry and spiritual thought. Mamani, I see you in the pages of this book.

And finally ...

> To my students and clients, for sharing their stories of their life journey with me. Forever these are etched in my heart.
>
> To my family and friends for their love and support throughout the many moons.
>
> And to each person whose encounter brought me insight and awakening.

I sit in thankfulness ...
humbled by the Hand of the Divine.

About the Author

Born into Iran's rich traditions of mysticism and poetry, Mitra Rahbar was awakened to her calling very early in life and soon after, embarked upon a mission of spirituality, service, and artistry. In 1978, Mitra was forced to emigrate, leaving behind her family and homeland. In the face of the trauma and decades-long hardships that followed, Mitra remained steadfast in her devotion and dedication to her mission.

Influenced by her mother, poet Mehrtaj Safai, as well as literary masters, Gibran, Saadi, and Hafez, Mitra has woven a unique tapestry, serving as a mystic, guide, teacher, healer, poet, and songstress for the last four decades.

In 2015, Mitra authored her first book, *Miraculous Silence: A Journey to Illumination and Healing Through Prayer* (Tarcher/Penguin Random House). In 2017, she founded *Servants of Love*—a training program for those called to a life of spiritual service.

For the last decade, Mitra has been active in raising funds and securing aid for educational and natural disaster relief efforts in Iran, Afghanistan, and other regions of the Middle East. Most recently, in 2024, she founded the Mehrtaj Safai Middle School, for girls from seven villages in the underserved, impoverished Iranian provinces of Sistan and Baluchestan.

Made in the USA
Columbia, SC
25 July 2024